200 EASY-TO-LEARN MAGICAL ILLUSIONS AMAZING PUZZLES & STUNNING STUNTS

200 EASY-TO-LEARN MAGICAL ILLUSIONS

AMAZING PUZZLES & STUNNING STUNTS

NICHOLAS EINHORN

PHOTOGRAPHY BY PAUL BRICKNELL

HERMES HOUSE

For my wife Joanne and our beautiful daughter Emily. I love you both with all my heart.

This edition is published by Hermes House, an imprint of Anness Publishing Ltd, Hermes House, 88–89 Blackfriars Road, London SE1 8HA; tel. 020 7401 2077; fax 020 7633 9499

www.hermeshouse.com; www.annesspublishing.com

If you like the images in this book and would like to investigate using them for publishing, promotions or advertising, please visit our website www.practicalpictures.com for more information.

ETHICAL TRADING POLICY
At Anness Publishing we believe that business should be conducted in an ethical and ecologically sustainable way, with respect for the environment and a proper regard to the replacement of the natural resources we employ.

As a publisher, we use a lot of wood pulp to make high-quality paper for printing, and that wood commonly comes from spruce trees. We are therefore currently growing more than 500,000 trees in two Scottish forest plantations near Aberdeen – Berrymoss (130 hectares/320 acres) and West Touxhill (125 hectares/305 acres). The forests we manage contain twice the number of trees employed each year in paper-making for our books.

Because of this ongoing ecological investment programme, you, as our customer, can have the pleasure and reassurance of knowing that a tree is being cultivated on your behalf to naturally replace the materials used to make the book you are holding.

Our forestry programme is run in accordance with the UK Woodland Assurance Scheme (UKWAS) and will be certified by the internationally recognized Forest Stewardship Council (FSC). The FSC is a non-government organization dedicated to promoting responsible management of the world's forests. Certification ensures forests are managed in an environmentally sustainable and socially responsible basis. For further information about this scheme, go to www.annesspublishing.com/trees

contents

close-up magic
10

party tricks
70

optical illusions
104

stunts and puzzles
124

stand-up magic
170

stage illusions
218

putting on a show
242

introduction

Let me start by reading your mind. You have already flicked through the pages of this book and looked at a few tricks before beginning to read this. Am I right? If you did, that's great! It shows a desire to learn, and if there is one thing that drives people to action it is desire.

I don't want you just to read this book: I want you to breathe life into the tricks that fill its pages. The fun is bursting to get out, and with a little help you can make it happen and in the process entertain and amaze your friends, family and whoever else is lucky enough to be around when you perform.

If this is the first magic book you have ever read then you are in for a treat. If you know a little bit about magic already, the contents will increase your magical knowledge and teach you a host of new tricks, puzzles and stunts to enjoy and share. The exciting thing about this collection of mysteries is that it won't cost you a small fortune to construct the props you'll need. You may already own most of the component parts; all you need to do is gather the relevant items together and assemble them in the correct order.

Inside this book there are over 200 secrets. They range from simple pranks, jokes and tricks you can play on your friends to the kind of stage illusions that you have probably seen master magicians performing on television. We all know that magicians never reveal their secrets, but why is that? Well, keeping secrets is how the art of magic has survived for over 4,000 years. If everyone knew how it was all done, the mystery would have been lost and magic would have died long ago. Instead, the ancient art is alive and thriving all over the world. In light of this, please help to keep the heart of magic beating by keeping the secrets you learn to yourself.

All the tricks in this book have one thing in common: they are incredibly simple to learn. However, just because a trick is easy to learn does not mean it is easy for your friends to figure out how it is done. Don't underestimate the impression these tricks and stunts will make on your friends. Some of my all-time favourite magic tricks are incredibly simple, and the amount of bafflement and entertainment that can be derived from them is out of proportion to the complexity of the method. If you learn tricks that are easy to execute, you can put most of your effort into making your performance fun and entertaining without having to remember too many special "moves" or worrying about getting the trick to work.

These tricks may be easy to learn, but that does not necessarily mean that they are easy to perform. There is a big difference between learning a trick in the privacy of your room and performing it convincingly in front of your friends, family or even a large audience of strangers. The only way to become really good at performing is to do it as often as possible. If you take every opportunity that comes your way you will soon develop a skill for building a rapport with your audience and creating a memorable moment of magic for both them and you, rather than just demonstrating a few clever tricks.

There are two ways to present magic. One is as a "wise guy", making fun of people in the audience to get cheap laughs at their expense and trying to prove that you can do something they can't. If you opt for this approach you can be certain that you will not be well received: instead of entertaining people you will probably have the reverse effect. On the other hand, if you adopt a more "inclusive" approach to your

Left: Making someone appear on stage is a common trick that is performed in large-scale stage illusions and can also be done at home.

Above: With just a balloon and a sharp stick, this young performer is able to perform a simple yet very effective piece of magic in front of an audience.

performance you can still make everyone laugh, but at no one's expense; rather than alienating your audience, you will be able to draw people towards you like a human magnet.

You are likely to find that almost everyone likes to watch *good* magic. If you are performing for a small group of people, don't be surprised if that small group starts to grow until you are surrounded by a much larger crowd of spectators. If you are going to rise to the challenge of performing to more people, you will need to know more than one or two tricks. The good news is that once you have learnt the secrets in this book you will be able to entertain people at the drop of a hat and will even be in a position to put together a full programme for a special event.

You are never too young or too old to start learning or performing magic. I began learning when I was four years old, but I know people who are over sixty and only just developing an interest in learning magic.

Watching magic also appeals to all ages. Of course, children love to be entertained and in one respect they are an easy audience, because they really believe in magic. However, in another way, entertaining a group of children is infinitely more demanding than engaging

Right: A close-up magician performing a card trick at a party will soon attract a small crowd of spectators who can sometimes take part in the tricks.

more knowing adults. Children are not a forgiving crowd, and if you don't have the ability to control your young audience they could end up controlling you. Adults, on the other hand, pose a different problem, since they need to be entertained with a certain level of sophistication. They must be treated as an intelligent group, and persuading them to suspend their disbelief can be a tough challenge.

This book begins with a section called Close-up Magic, which is by far the most popular type of magic among amateur magicians. This is because it is accessible to everyone. It requires only the simplest of props: with a collection of inexpensive everyday objects it is possible to perform a host of magic tricks that are very often just as impressive as those you would pay large sums for at a magic store.

Party Tricks will teach you fun things to try out on your friends and incorporate into your magic repetoire to help create a more interesting, entertaining and intriguing presentation. Most of them are fairly easy to learn and perform and require just a few props, so many can be improptu gags.

This book contains more than just magic tricks, and there is a good reason for this. Besides knowing the secrets, a good magician needs to appreciate how our minds can play tricks on us, and the chapter on Optical Illusions shows how we can be made to see things in different ways. You will be amazed as printed images seem to move and two-dimensional drawings seem to change from one size to another.

The chapter called Stunts and Puzzles will enable you to set up challenges for your friends to solve, and unless they have read this book or seen the puzzles before, the chances are that it will take quite a bit of time and lateral thinking before they find the solutions. These puzzles test people's ability to look at a situation from many angles and to use problem-solving techniques to find the solutions. (Incidentally, this is excellent practice if you ever want to try inventing your own magic tricks.)

In the Stand-up Magic chapter you'll find tricks that you can do in front of a bigger audience. While many of these would also work for a smaller crowd, they are similar in style to the tricks performed by magicians as part of a stage show. Often this means that you will use larger props, but it does not mean it will cost you a lot of money. Once again, you will find that many of the items required can either be found at home or purchased inexpensively from a local store.

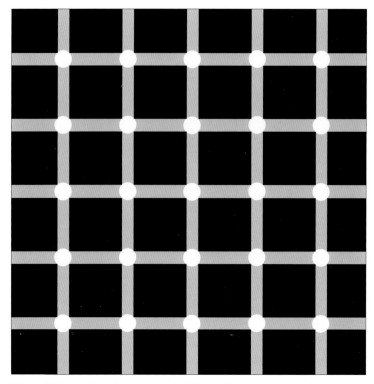

Above: Take a look at the above optical illusion. Do you see black dots jumping around inside the white circles? The Optical Illusions chapter is full of fun images that move, change and play with your visual perception.

Finally, the Stage Illusions chapter explains how to construct and perform some amazing illusions that you might use as part of a bigger show to make it seem more professional – you can learn how to make people appear, vanish, shrink and even float.

No matter how large or small a magic trick is, there are two overriding elements that govern its success: method and presentation. Even if you intend to learn only a few basic tricks it is vital that you understand the importance of these two essential ingredients.

In the context of magic, "method" is another word for "secret". Your audience should never be aware of the method during your performance; to be sure of this you must practise the tricks until you know the method back to front so that there is no chance that you will give the method away. When you start a trick the last thing you should be worrying about is how it works – it should be smooth and natural so that you can concentrate on your patter and other aspects of the overall performance. If you find this thought popping into your mind during a performance, you have not rehearsed enough.

Left: In the Stunts and Puzzles chapter you will learn many tricks, including how to defy the law of gravity by making a paper tube held together with paper clips climb up a piece of string.

Above: In the Stage Magic chapter you will learn how to construct a special magic prop called a Square Circle Production. This can be used to make any number of things appear and disappear.

Presentation is everything that surrounds the method, and in a sense it is everything the audience *is* aware of. It is what carries the trick from the beginning to the end. The presentation incorporates your patter, which can be made up of jokes or banter, or a story that you weave in with the magic. You may choose a more serious presentation if you wish to create the illusion of being a mind reader or someone who can influence other people's actions and control their minds. Whatever presentation you opt for, make sure you have rehearsed it thoroughly. A trick that seems really simple to do may in fact be more difficult to perform successfully than you imagine. The secret of success in the magic business is practice.

If you are ready to learn a great magic trick that will probably fool even you the first time you try it, find a cotton handkerchief or table napkin and then turn to the description for Vanishing Coin in Handkerchief. Once you've tried it out you'll probably agree that it is a great trick and you'll also see that

Right: Hiring a magician for a group of excited children at a festival or birthday party is a great way to keep them entertained as well as introducing them to magic. Many of the world's top magicians first started learning magic after being introduced to it at a party at a very young age. However, many adults enjoy magic too, and you are never too old to start learning how to perform it.

learning magic from a book is an interesting experience: until you perform a trick you just don't know how good it looks.

This book aims to make learning tricks and illusions as easy and enjoyable as possible. Over 1,300 photographs show every stage of every trick, and the accompanying descriptions explain anything that may not be immediately obvious from the pictures. If, after learning these tricks, you have the desire to go even further, take a look at Where to Learn More, which contains sources of information that can help you progress to the next level.

One last piece of advice: you may find that setting yourself a deadline encourages you to assemble a small number of tricks into a simple yet effective routine. Perhaps you have a child or a friend who is having a birthday party, and you could perform a small show to help them celebrate. Perhaps a local group is staging a variety show to raise money for a charity. If so, volunteer yourself as one of the acts.

Knowing you have to be ready by a certain date will spur you on to find the type of tricks that you think would entertain a specific audience and give you the ultimate reason to dive in. You never know, this could be the start of a lifelong journey in magic. I hope that you enjoy this collection of curiosities and wish you good luck with your newfound hobby.

close-up magic

In this chapter you will find over 40 magic tricks. Most of these routines use ordinary objects that can be found around the house, and several of them can be performed without any preparation at all. While some use simple sleight-of-hand, others require a minimum amount of skill. Once you have learnt a few of these close-up tricks, you'll be able to perform to an audience in no time.

introduction

Performed directly in front of the spectator, close-up magic uses small, familiar props such as banknotes, coins, handkerchiefs, pens, fruit, keys, playing cards, string, and lots more besides. As soon as magicians learnt to manipulate these small objects they began using them in tricks, although the term "close-up magic" did not come into use until the 20th century, when its rise in popularity was assisted by several magicians who inspired a generation of magic artistry.

Dai Vernon (1894–1992) was a Canadian-born magician who moved to the USA and worked as a silhouette cutter before his magic began to impress all who saw him. Early in his career he baffled Harry Houdini, who used to boast that he could not be fooled, with one of his sleight-of-hand tricks. Even though he repeated it over and over again (some say seven times) Houdini could not see how Vernon accomplished his miracle. During the 1960s Vernon moved to Los Angeles to spend as much time as

Above: Ricky Jay is of the world's finest exponents of sleight-of-hand. He is also an established actor and has appeared in many classic films, including as the villain Henry Gupta in the James Bond blockbuster *Tomorrow Never Dies*.

possible at the Magic Castle in Hollywood, and people travelled from all over the world in the hope of spending even a small amount of time with this master of magic, who became affectionately known as "The Professor". His most famous tricks were his versions of the classic Chinese Linking Rings and the legendary Cups and Balls. The urn containing his ashes remains on display at the Magic Castle, and he will always be one of the most important names in magic's history.

The Expert at the Card Table by S. W. Erdnase, published in 1902, explained many previously unknown card moves and secret ways of cheating at card games. The biggest mystery of all, however, is the identity of the author, since S. W. Erdnase never existed. Spelling the name backwards gives E. S. Andrews, which could be a clue, but to this day no one knows who really wrote the work.

This revolutionary book gave fresh insights to many card tricks and among the many people who may have been inspired was Ed Marlo (1913–91). Marlo could perform magic with all kinds of objects but specialized in playing cards. His techniques were so far ahead of their time that he quickly became a major authority in his chosen area, publishing over 2,000 of his sleights and tricks. It is worth noting that many gambling cheats have used similar moves, and in the early 20th century crooked gamblers and magicians sometimes exchanged ideas. In fact, Dai Vernon searched extensively for notorious card cheats in order to learn their secrets and apply them to his magic tricks.

Another legendary name in close-up magic is Tony Slydini (1901–91). Originally from Italy, this famous magician moved to the USA around 1930 and was the East Coast's answer to Dai Vernon. Slydini was a master of misdirection and applied layers of psychology to his magic to enhance his illusions. He was one of the first to teach his use of psychology as part of his overall strategy for bringing out the artistry in magic, and his methods are still used and respected today. One of his most important messages was to *be natural* when executing a sleight. Your hand may be secretly holding a coin, but if you hold your hand in a natural way no one will guess. Of course, when you think about doing this it is actually quite difficult: if you try too hard it inevitably looks unnatural. Try it. Rest a coin on the tips of your curled fingers and hold your hand in such a way that it looks empty. Not easy, is it?

Left: Tommy Wonder was a superb magician and inventor. His creativity and originality were unparalleled and he was one of the most popular acts to be seen at magic conventions all over the world.

Right: Michael Ammar is a former FISM winner. He has worked as a magic consultant for David Copperfield, Siegfried & Roy, Doug Henning and even Michael Jackson. He has written several books and is one of the most popular magicians on the worldwide magic lecture circuit.

Slydini inspired a whole generation of magicians to increase the power of their magic by acting naturally and applying psychology. In a sense, his work is the antithesis of the popular notion that the hand is quicker than the eye. Slow moves can be just as deceptive if they are performed well.

Today, close-up magic is the most popular area of magic. This is because it costs very little to learn a simple trick – the only real investment is time – and opportunities to perform are increasing. In an age in which people frequently spend vast sums on entertaining there is scope to make a decent wage performing close-up magic at private parties and corporate events.

Advances in techniques and technology over the past 50 years have led to a massive growth in the magic industry. Almost daily there are new tricks to learn and buy, but far too many are simply poor copies or so-called improvements of existing tricks.

The reality is that many are not improvements at all, but backward steps. It is too easy for anyone to blitz the magic fraternity with a never-ending stream of inferior products. But while hobbyists and even some professionals are happy to perform tricks using specially made gimmicks in place of sleight-of-hand, there are still those who prefer to do things the old-fashioned way.

There are many brilliant close-up magicians around the world today. It would be impossible to name them all, but among the most respected are Ricky Jay, Bill Malone, Michael Ammar and David Roth from the USA, Juan Tamariz from Spain, Guy Hollingworth from Britain, Lennart Green from Sweden and, until his death, Holland's Tommy Wonder.

Every three years the world's finest magicians gather at a convention called FISM (Fédération Internationale des Sociétés Magiques). Held in a different country each time, this is the Olympics of the magic world. Among the most exciting events are the competitions, at which the top talents compete for the FISM Grand Prix. Competing in The Hague in 2003 was one of the most nerve-wracking experiences of my own performing career. I was placed joint second in the micro magic category with Shawn Farquhar from Canada. The winner was America's Jason Latimer.

Some of the greatest magicians in the world will have performed many of the wonderful magic tricks in this chapter. Now it is your turn to learn them and begin your journey as a close-up magician. Practise hard and – who knows? – maybe *you* will be a future FISM award winner. After all, everybody has to start somewhere.

magnetic money

This is a very quick trick that can be performed at a moment's notice. Two banknotes are shown on both sides, then laid together on the table in a criss-cross fashion and rubbed on the tablecloth as if to create "static electricity". The top note is lifted up and, incredibly, the lower note seems to adhere to it as if magnetized. The notes are then separated and given out for examination.

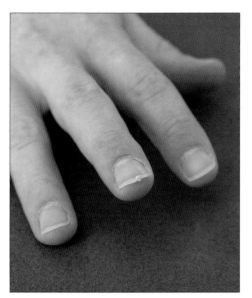

1 You will need a tiny piece of reusable putty adhesive, which you stick on the tip of your middle finger. Display two banknotes or borrow them from a spectator. This trick works best with fairly new, crisp notes. They should have a design with some colouring similar to the putty somewhere in the middle.

secret view

2 As you take the banknotes, stick the putty to the centre of one of them. It will be almost invisible, and will certainly not be noticed by the spectators if the note is glanced at casually.

3 Lay the note with the putty on the table and place the other note crossways on top of it. The piece of putty will be sandwiched in the middle.

4 Secretly squeeze the notes together so they stick to one another as you rub them over the surface of the table, supposedly to create the static electricity.

5 Bring the notes back to the centre of the table and slowly lift the upper note by the ends.

6 As you slowly raise the upper note the lower note will adhere to it and lift off the table.

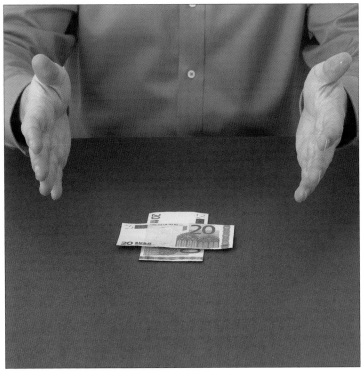

7 Release both notes and allow them to drop back to the surface of the table.

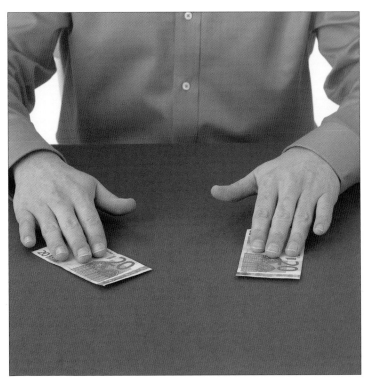

8 Separate the notes and rub them on the table again, apparently to discharge the static.

secret view

9 As you pick up the notes from the table, secretly scrape off the putty with your right middle finger.

10 Finally, hand out the banknotes to the spectators for examination. There will be nothing to find.

pen-go

A pen is wrapped up in a piece of paper and the paper is slowly torn into pieces, the pen having vanished into thin air! Actually it doesn't disappear into thin air – it flies up your sleeve, but no one sees it go.

The pen is on a special gimmick known to magicians as a "pull". It's best to use this trick as part of a longer sequence or routine that requires the spectator to write something.

1 Attach the lid of a pen to a piece of elastic approximately 30cm (12in) long (depending on the length of your arm). At the other end tie a safety pin. You will also need a piece of paper a little longer then the pen.

secret view

2 Fasten the pin inside the top of your right sleeve, so that when the elastic is loose the pen hangs just below your elbow. When you are ready to begin you will need to pull the pen down your sleeve secretly and hold it by the lid. Pull the pen out of the lid when handing it out for use. When it is returned, re-cap the pen, ensuring the elastic stays hidden behind your right wrist.

secret view

3 Begin to wrap the paper around the pen, making sure that the elastic is still hidden from view from the front. This picture shows the starting position as seen from behind, with the pen at one corner of the paper.

4 From the spectators' point of view the elastic is completely hidden by the back of your hand.

secret view

5 Wrap up the pen by rolling the paper loosely around it.

secret view

6 Hold the pen and paper loosely in your right hand.

secret view

7 Allow the pen to slip out of the paper and up your sleeve. The tube of paper will hold its shape.

8 Rip the paper tube in half and then tear it into smaller pieces. Finally, throw the pieces of paper up in the air for a dramatic finish.

let there be light

You show the spectators an ordinary light bulb, which you then screw into your empty fist where it immediately begins to glow. After a few seconds it "switches" off and you hand the light bulb to the spectators *so that they can check it has not been prepared in any way. You show your empty hands and take your well-deserved applause. This trick also requires a "pull".*

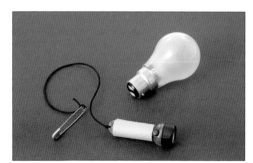

1 Prepare a pull by tying one end of a piece of elastic approximately 30cm (12in) long (depending on the length of your arm) to a safety pin and the other end to a miniature flashlight. The flashlight needs to be one that operates at the push of a button rather than with a switch that needs to be pushed up or down. You will also require a frosted light bulb.

secret view

2 Fasten the pin inside the top of your right sleeve so that when the elastic is loose the flashlight hangs just below your elbow. Hand the light bulb out for examination. Meanwhile, secretly position the flashlight in your right hand, as shown above. It is important that you practise doing this in such a way that no one sees what you are doing.

3 Retrieve the light bulb from the audience and hold it in your right hand, as shown. Show everyone that your left hand is empty and then hold it in a fist under the bulb.

secret view

4 This secret view shows how the tip of the flashlight is resting against the side of the light bulb. From the front the audience will not be able to tell what is really happening.

5 Slowly pretend to screw the bulb into your left hand. As you do so, activate the flashlight by covertly pushing the button with the fingers of your right hand. The bulb will glow just as if it were screwed into a light fitting.

6 Unscrew the light bulb from your fist, meanwhile turning off the flashlight, and show that your left hand is still empty.

secret view

7 As you are showing your left hand, release the flashlight from your right hand, allowing it to shoot up your sleeve and out of sight.

8 Finally open both hands wide, showing the audience that there are no secret gadgets to be seen in your hands.

tip *This could also make a great stage trick, and if you wear the special pull at all times you can even remove a bulb from a table lamp to do the trick at a moment's notice. Of course, if you do this you must make sure the lamp is switched off and unplugged before you remove the bulb and always replace it afterwards. Also remember that if the light has been on for a while the bulb will be extremely hot!*

coin through coaster

A glass is covered with a drinks coaster and a coin is visibly caused to pass through the coaster and into the glass. Performed properly, the illusion of the coin melting through the coaster is perfect. This is *perhaps one of the most challenging tricks in this book, but the effect is worth the effort. You will need a glass, a coaster, two identical coins and several hours to practise and make the moves flow smoothly.*

secret view

1 Secretly hold a coin on the fingertips of your right hand and pick up the coaster with your left hand.

2 Cover the coin with the coaster so that you are holding both the coin and the coaster in your right hand.

3 Now you need to learn a move that enables you to show both sides of the coaster without revealing the coin. As you turn your hand over to show the reverse side of the coaster, bend the fingers in, sliding the coin back so that as much of the coaster as possible is visible. Then turn your hand back, reversing the sliding motion.

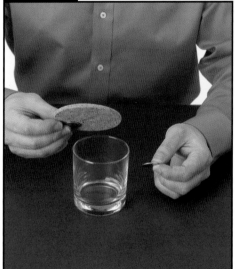

secret view

4 Display the second coin in the fingertips of your left hand and simultaneously move the coaster towards the top of the glass. The coin under the coaster is shown here, but it must remain hidden when you perform the trick.

5 Tap the visible coin against the side of the glass as you lay the coaster on top, secretly trapping the hidden coin between the rim of the glass and the coaster. The noise from the tapping will cover any noise the hidden coin makes as it touches the rim.

6 Show the visible coin being held between the finger and thumb of your right hand, while your left hand holds the coaster in place on the glass.

7 With the coin between the finger and thumb of your right hand, tap it against the coaster three times. After the third tap, squeeze the coin, flipping it sideways and pinching it so that it is hidden behind the right fingers. (This is called a "pinch vanish".) At the same moment, lift the coaster at the back with your left thumb to disengage the coin, which is then seen and heard to clink into the glass.

8 This picture shows how things look from your side at the moment when the coin apparently penetrates the coaster.

9 As soon as you hear the coin clink into the glass lift the coaster off the glass with your left hand.

10 Transfer the coaster to your right hand, placing it over the hidden coin, and tip the visible coin out of the glass on to the table.

11 Finally, place the coaster on the table (leaving the hidden coin underneath) and display both hands to show that they are empty.

ring on a string

A ring penetrates a piece of string, the ends of which are both in view throughout the manoeuvre. This trick requires a ring, a safety pin and a handkerchief. It has its roots in an effect called "Sefalaljia", which was created by Stewart James.

1 Show a length of string approximately 45cm (18in) long and lay it on the table. Borrow a ring or use your own. Lay it next to the centre of the string. Then explain that by using a safety pin you can make it look as if the ring is actually threaded on the string.

2 Cover the middle of the string with a handkerchief. Make sure both ends are clearly in view.

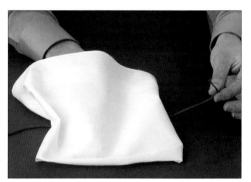

secret view

3 Under the handkerchief, push a small loop of the string through the ring.

secret view

4 Push the safety pin through the string and pin the left side of the loop to the string to the left of the ring, as shown. This will leave you with the loop marked with an "x" above.

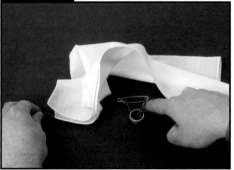

secret view

5 Put the first finger of your right hand into the loop and hold the left end of the string with your left hand.

6 This is what it looks like from the front. Explain that the ring can't really be on the string, as the ends have not been out of sight.

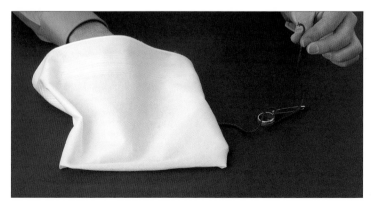

7 Pull the string to the left while keeping your right finger pinned to the table. The string will be pulled through the ring. This is covered by the handkerchief.

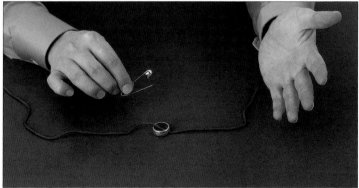

8 Finally, remove the handkerchief, undo the pin and show that the ring really is on the string.

Chinese coin off string

A Chinese coin with a hole in it is threaded on to a length of string. A spectator holds both ends of the string, and yet you are able to remove the coin. This is a perfect follow-up to Ring on a String. You will see that the two tricks can easily be incorporated into a routine.

1 You need a piece of string, a handkerchief and two identical Chinese coins with holes in the middle (or you can use two matching rings instead). Hide one of the coins in your right hand: your audience must be aware of only one coin throughout the trick.

2 Thread the visible coin on to the string and have a spectator hold both ends.

secret view

3 Cover the coin on the string with a handkerchief. This view shows the hidden duplicate coin concealed in your right hand.

secret view

4 Under cover of the handkerchief (which has been removed here for clarity) pull the centre of the cord through the hole in the middle of the loose coin.

secret view

5 Now pass this loop over the coin so that the coin hangs as shown.

secret view

6 Hide the original, threaded coin in your hand and slide it to the right, pulling the handkerchief over as you do so.

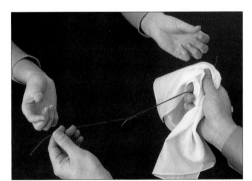

7 Slide both hands to the ends of the string: your spectator will let go. Allow the coin hidden in your right hand to slip off the cord, as you say, "Don't let go of the ends!"

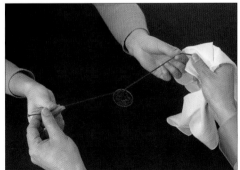

8 The spectator will take hold of the ends again, but the original threaded coin is now off the string and hidden under the handkerchief. ▶

tip *The success of this trick relies on the spectator letting go of the cord at stage 7 looking like an error on their part. Don't ask them to let go, simply make it happen by moving your hands. As soon as it occurs (allowing the hidden coin to slip off), make a big deal of the fact that they mustn't let go and get them to hold on again. If you can make this moment look natural and keep the second coin hidden, this is a very baffling trick.*

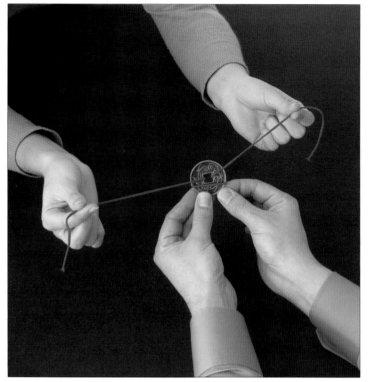

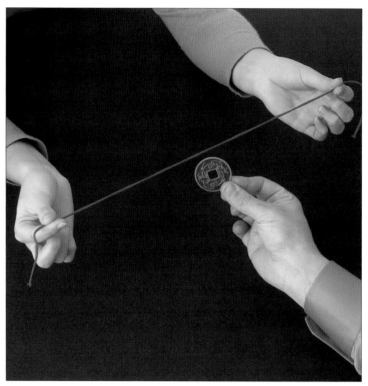

9 Put the handkerchief and the hidden coin in your pocket or to one side, keeping the coin concealed, then slowly untie the simple knot that holds the coin on the string.

10 Finish by showing that the coin has magically passed through the string.

rising ring on pencil

A borrowed ring is placed over a pencil that is held vertically by the magician. Slowly and eerily the ring begins to climb the pencil until it reaches the top. Considering how easy this trick is to do, it is incredibly effective and will fool most people.

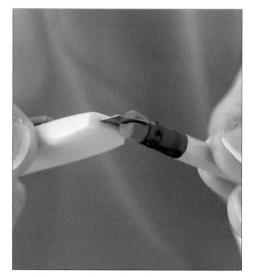

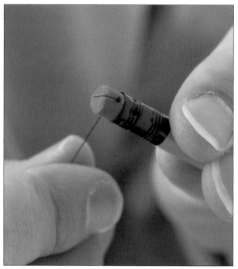

1 To set up the trick, take a pencil with an eraser on the end and with a sharp knife carefully make a slit in the middle of the eraser.

2 Take a length of very thin fishing line or thread (the thinnest you can find) and tie a small knot in one end, wedging this knot into the slit. (Thick black thread was used in these pictures so that you can see how the trick works.)

3 Attach the other end of the thread to a safety pin and fasten the pin to your belt loop or waistband. The thread should be approximately 50cm (20in) long, but you will need to experiment to find a length that suits you.

4 Put the pencil into your breast pocket. Carrying it in this
fashion means the thread will not get in the way.

5 Remove the pencil from your pocket, borrow a ring and drop
the ring over the top of the pencil and the thread. The fine
thread will remain unseen.

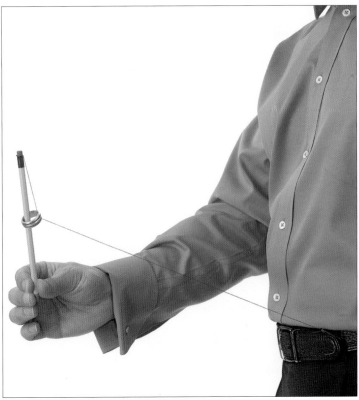

6 Make a magical gesture with your left hand while you slowly
move the pencil away from you, tightening the thread. The
ring will rise up the pencil.

7 When the ring reaches the top remove it and hand it back to
the owner. Either replace the pencil in your pocket or move
the pencil away from you, secretly pulling the thread out of the
eraser in order to use the pencil for something else.

gravity-defying ring

A rubber band is broken and a borrowed ring is threaded on to it. The band is held between both hands at an angle of approximately 45 degrees. The ring slides up to the top of the band, uncannily defying the laws of gravity. You must try this out, as it is one of the most convincing illusions you are ever likely to see; the first time I saw it I was completely fooled.

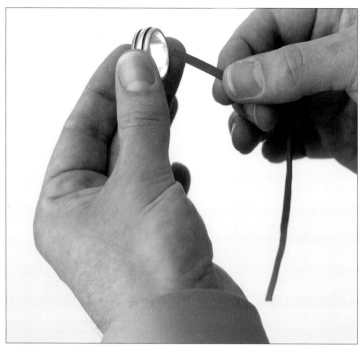

1 Choose a medium-sized rubber band with no imperfections, and break it. Hold the ring in the fingertips of your left hand and insert the top 2cm (¾in) of the band through the ring.

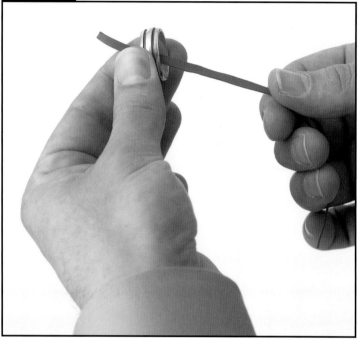

secret view

2 Notice how the band is pinched between the left forefinger and thumb, with the back of the hand towards the spectators, while the ring also remains pinched.

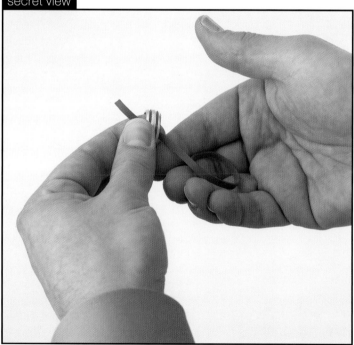

secret view

3 Now pinch the band just under the ring with your right finger and thumb.

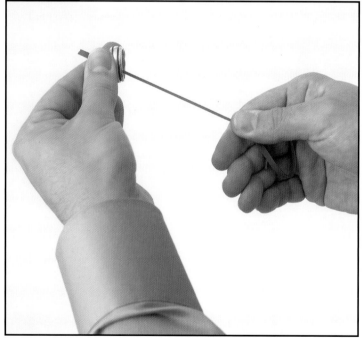

secret view

4 Pull the band taut. Most of the band is hidden in your right hand.

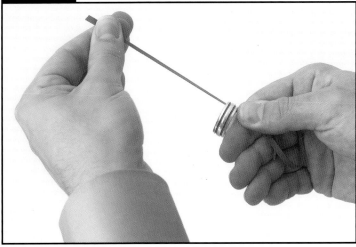

5 Allow the ring to drop down the band to rest on the index finger of your right hand.

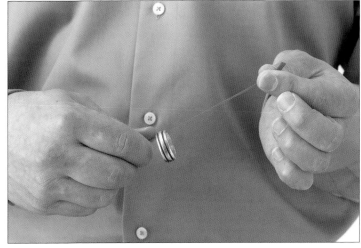

6 From the front it looks as if you are holding the band by the two ends. In fact, what the spectators are seeing is about 2cm (¾in) of the band stretched to look like the entire band.

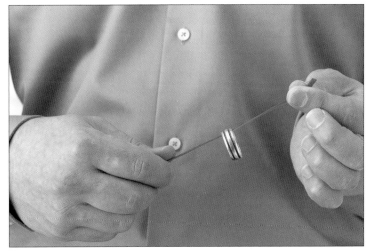

7 Hold the band at an angle of 45 degrees and slowly release the pressure of the right finger and thumb. The ring will adhere to the band and as the band retracts the illusion is that the ring is climbing up the band.

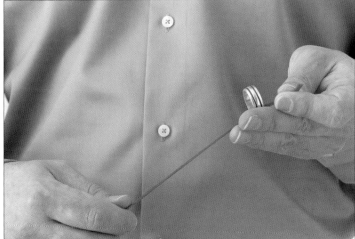

8 As soon as the band has been allowed to retract as much as possible the fingers of the left hand complete the illusion by reaching for the ring, sliding it off the band and handing it back to the owner.

9 Finish by displaying the ring and the band held in your fingertips and handing them out for examination.

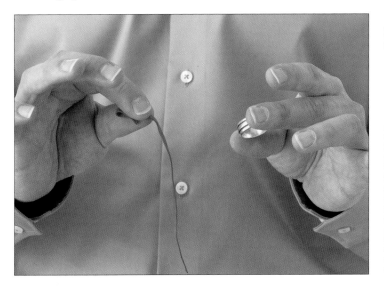

tip *The band must be released slowly and smoothly for the ring to climb steadily. Experiment with different thicknesses and sizes of rubber band, as some work better than others for this trick. The weight of the ring can also make a difference, so try using different ones, then use the combination of ring and rubber band that works best.*

dissolving coin (version 1)

A borrowed, marked coin is covered with a handkerchief and dropped inside a glass of water. The spectators can hear the coin plop as it enters the water, yet when the handkerchief is removed, the coin has gone. The marked coin can then be discovered in a variety of ways.

For this trick you will need a small glass disc: the glass of an old wristwatch would work perfectly. You will also need a glass of water and a handkerchief. Ask someone in the audience to mark a coin with a pen so that they will be able to recognize it later.

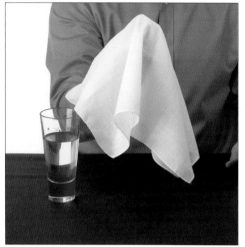

1 Hold a handkerchief by one corner with your left hand, with the glass disc secretly hidden under the fingertips behind the handkerchief.

2 Place the coin under the handkerchief, and as your right hand comes close to the left one allow the coin to fall into your fingers as shown, while simultaneously positioning the glass disc in the coin's place.

3 Hold the glass disc up under the handkerchief so that its outline can be seen through the material. Everyone will think this is the coin.

4 Take hold of the handkerchief with your left hand and position it over the glass of water. The coin is still held secretly in the right hand. Let the disc drop into the water with a plop.

5 Pull the handkerchief away using your right hand, making sure that the coin is adequately covered by the handkerchief.

6 The coin has vanished. You can even let the spectators look straight down into the glass and they will see nothing.

tip *To reproduce the marked coin at the start of the trick (which will then be hidden in your right hand) you can reach into a spectator's pocket and reveal the coin, creating the illusion that it somehow travelled across time and space invisibly, or you may want to use it to perform Marked Coin in Ball of Wool.*

dissolving coin (version 2)

Here is a different method for what is essentially the same trick. A coin (marked if desired) is dropped into a glass of acid, which *instantly dissolves it. Do not perform both versions of this trick in the same act. Try out both, and then perform the one you prefer.*

1 You will need a tall glass, a coin, a handkerchief and a bottle of water with a label that suggests that the contents are dangerous.

2 Pour some of the liquid from the bottle into the glass, explaining that it is a very strong acid that will dissolve anything it touches (except for glass, of course!).

3 Show the coin to the audience and hold it in the centre of the handkerchief with your right hand. Pick up the glass with your left hand. Notice how the glass is held.

4 Move the handkerchief over the glass and position the coin above it.

secret view

5 This secret view shows how the glass is tipped forwards and how the coin is actually positioned behind it. Let the coin fall in the direction of the arrow.

secret view

6 As the coin falls it will hit the side of the glass before resting in your left hand. The spectators will hear the coin hit the glass and assume it went inside.

7 As this shot from the front shows, the spectators cannot see that the coin is now in your left hand.

secret view

8 As you pick up the edge of the handkerchief to remove it from the glass, secretly pick up the coin from the palm of your left hand using the fingertips of your right hand.

9 With the coin now hidden under the handkerchief you can remove the handkerchief from the glass completely to show that the coin has vanished, and explain that the acid has dissolved it.

coin through ring

A coin is placed under a thick handkerchief. The corners of the handkerchief are gathered together and threaded through a finger *ring smaller than the coin, securing the coin inside. The magician causes the coin to pass through the handkerchief, freeing the ring.*

secret view

1 Hold a handkerchief by one corner in your left hand and a coin in the fingertips of your right hand.

2 Cover your right hand and the coin with the handkerchief, and remove your left hand.

3 Secretly gather a pinch of material at the back of the coin. This pinch is held with the thumb of your right hand.

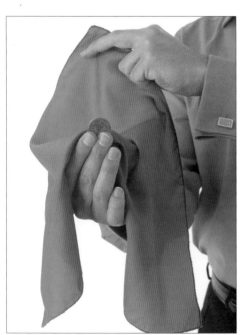

secret view

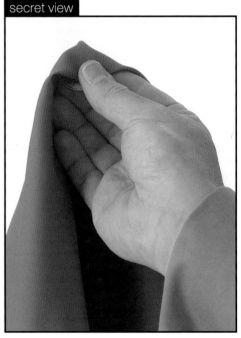

4 Raise the front of the handkerchief with your left hand to show the coin underneath. At the same time secretly grip the back of the handkerchief between the thumb and forefinger of your left hand.

5 Cover the coin again with the handkerchief, but secretly carry both layers of the handkerchief forward.

6 This close-up view shows that the coin is now really on the outside of the handkerchief.

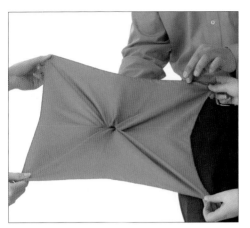

7 Twist the handkerchief several times under the coin. The fabric will twist around, hiding the ring.

8 Ask someone to hold on to the coin through the handkerchief. If you keep the "open" side downwards no one will suspect the coin is actually on the outside. Gather the four corners of the handkerchief and thread them through a finger ring, pushing it up to the coin.

9 Take back the covered coin from the first person and ask two people to hold two corners each and stretch out the handkerchief, as shown.

10 Reach underneath the handkerchief and remove the coin from within the folds.

11 This picture shows from underneath how the coin is removed from the folds of the handkerchief.

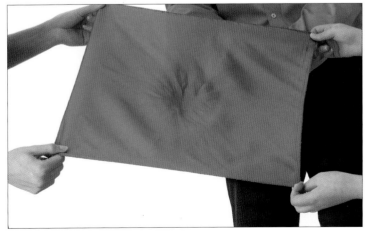

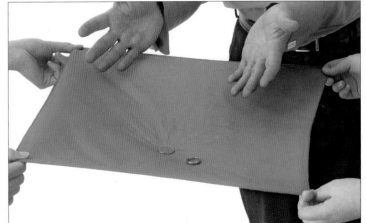

12 Release the coin and the ring so that the two people are left holding only the empty handkerchief.

13 Finish the trick by tossing both the ring and the coin on to the stretched-out handkerchief.

vanishing coin in handkerchief

A coin is clearly seen wrapped in the centre of a handkerchief. With a magical gesture the handkerchief is pulled open to reveal that the coin has completely vanished. This simple and impromptu trick is one

of the very best you could ever learn. Try it now and you will amaze yourself, as the coin seems to disappear into thin air! It is one of the few tricks where the secret is almost as amazing as the trick itself.

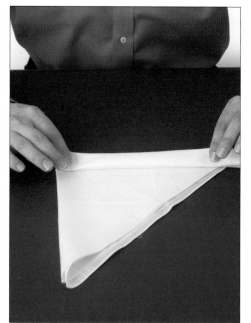

1 Lay a handkerchief in front of you in the shape of a diamond. Place a coin just a tiny bit to the left of the centre.

2 Fold the bottom half up to meet the top and pick up the right hand corner of the triangle that is formed.

3 Now fold the right side over to meet the left. The coin should not move during either of these folds.

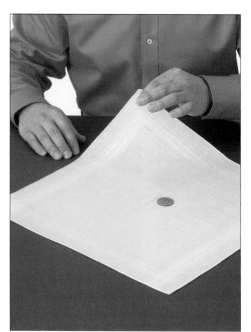

4 Pinch the coin inside the handkerchief with your right hand and slowly turn the coin over and over, rolling up the handkerchief as you do so.

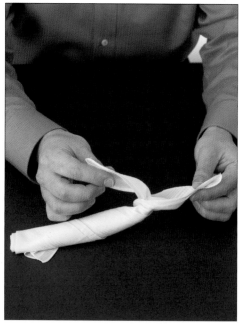

5 Continue rolling up the handkerchief until you reach the top.

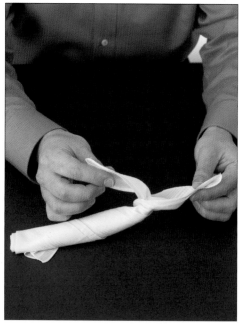

6 Grip the two pointed ends, one in each hand, and slowly pull them apart.

7 The coin has vanished! Actually it is inside a secret fold, but no one would ever guess.

8 Tilt the left side of the handkerchief up so that the coin secretly runs down into your right fingers.

secret view

9 This is an exposed view of the coin once it has landed. Notice how it sits on the fingertips.

10 Bunch the handkerchief into your right hand, covering the coin. You can finish by placing the handkerchief and coin in your pocket.

the Bermuda triangle

Three pencils are laid on the table in the shape of a triangle. A small ship placed in the middle and covered with a glass mysteriously disappears, as does the glass. The whole trick is presented as a demonstration of how things seem to disappear inside the famous Bermuda triangle. This trick is actually two tricks put together. You can do just the first part if you wish, but running the two together makes a really great routine. The story about the Bermuda triangle turns a basic trick into an engaging presentation.

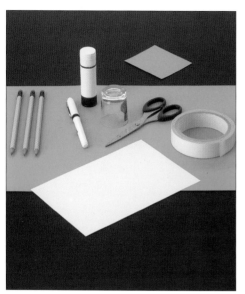

1 To set up the trick you will need several sheets of card (stock), three pencils, glue, double-sided adhesive tape, scissors, a pen, a glass and a sheet of paper.

2 Draw around the top of the glass on the card and cut out a disc that exactly matches the size of the rim.

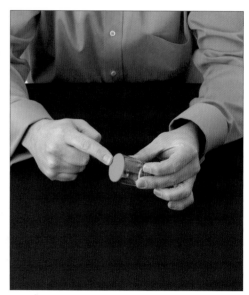

3 Glue this to the rim of the glass, making sure that no edges stick out. This special addition to the glass is known as a "gimmick".

4 Place a small piece of double-sided tape in the middle of the the card disc and press down firmly.

5 Draw a small ship on another piece of card and carefully cut it out using a pair of scissors. The ship must be smaller than the surface area of the base of the glass you are using.

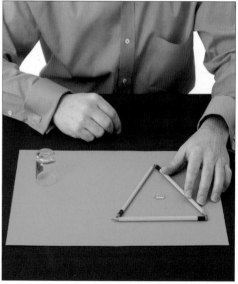

6 To set up the trick, arrange three pencils in a triangle on a piece of card that is exactly the same colour as your gimmick and place the ship in the middle. Place the glass, mouth down, on the card. (Notice how the gimmick becomes invisible.) Tell your spectators the legend that anything passing through the Bermuda triangle disappears.

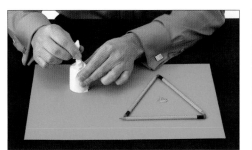

7 Take a sheet of plain paper and, being sure to keep the glass absolutely flat on the table, cover it as shown. The paper should not be wrapped too tightly around the glass.

8 Grip the glass through the paper and place both on top of the ship in the middle of the triangle.

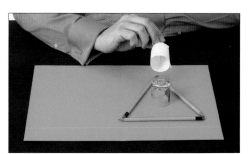

9 Lift up the paper, leaving the glass on the table. The ship will have totally disappeared from view, perfectly hidden by the gimmick on the bottom of the glass. Explain that the glass represents a tornado passing through the Bermuda triangle, and that when the tornado was directly over the ship it disappeared.

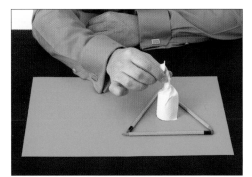

10 Re-cover the glass with the paper, then lift up the glass, gripping it through the paper. The ship will stick to the double-sided tape on the gimmick and will be lifted up with the glass.

11 Explain that when the tornado moved away the ship was never seen again. Notice how the glass has been moved near the back edge of the table. While you are speaking, secretly allow the glass to slip out of the paper and into your lap. These are examples of techniques called misdirection and lapping.

12 The paper will retain the shape of the glass, even though it is no longer covering the glass. Replace this empty shell in the centre of the triangle, explaining that hurricanes sometimes come back.

13 Slam your hand down on the paper, flattening it and revealing that the glass has disappeared! Pick up the paper and explain that even a tornado can disappear in the Bermuda triangle.

14 If you have a small box of props on a chair to your side you can secretly take the glass off your lap and put it away as you pick up the other props from the table. Be sure to hold the sheet of card so that it masks the glass being secretly removed from your lap.

tip *You must practise the misdirection and lapping until you can do it without thinking about it or making it obvious.*

magic papers

A piece of folded coloured paper is opened to reveal inside it another folded paper of a different colour; this too is opened to reveal another folded paper, and this in turn is found to contain a last folded paper. When the smallest piece of paper is unfolded fully, a small coin is placed inside. The coloured papers are re-folded, a magic spell is cast and when the papers are opened once again, the contents have changed into a coin of a much larger denomination. This is handed back to the surprised and very happy donor. You will need several different-coloured sheets of paper for this trick. A pair of scissors or a guillotine is also required to cut the paper to size. Using the magic papers you can also make coins appear and vanish, as well as change their denomination.

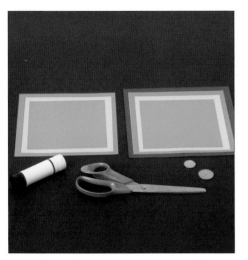

1 Using scissors, cut out a 20cm (8in) square of red paper. Cut out two 18cm (7in) squares of blue paper, two 16cm (6¼in) squares of yellow paper and two 14cm (5½in) squares of green paper.

2 Starting with a green square, fold the paper twice, to create three equal sections, as shown.

3 Fold this strip into three equal sections. Repeat these folds with each of the other papers. Make sure that the folds are neatly done and that the creases are sharp. When each paper is unfolded it should be divided into nine equal squares.

4 Carefully glue the two blue papers back to back so that they are joined at their centres, as shown.

tip *The best way to end the trick is to give the larger value coin to the person who lent you the small one.*

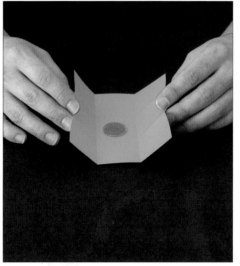

5 Place a coin of high denomination in the centre of a green square and wrap it up inside the paper, along the folds you made earlier. Place this green packet in the centre of a yellow paper and fold it inside. Finally, place the yellow paper inside the blue and fold the blue paper around it.

6 Now assemble the other papers by laying the red paper down first, followed by the (double) blue paper, with the hidden packet containing the coin of high denomination underneath, as shown.

7 Now place the yellow paper on top of the blue and the last green paper on top of the yellow. Fold each one inside the other to complete the set-up.

8 To perform the trick, show the packet of folded paper and a coin of low denomination. (Borrow this coin from a spectator if possible.)

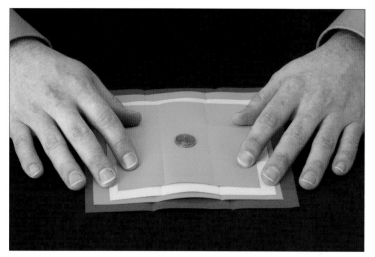

9 Open the nest of papers (being careful not to reveal the underside of the prepared blue sheet) and place the low-value coin in the centre of the green paper. Wrap the coin up in the green paper, then wrap this in each of the other papers in turn.

10 Secretly turn the blue paper over as you make the final fold in it.

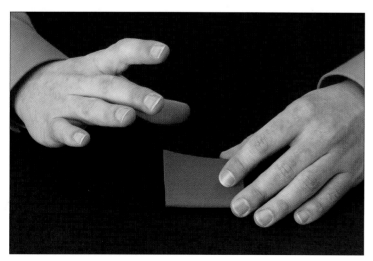

11 Wrap the blue paper up in the red paper, and cast a "mystic shadow" over the packet.

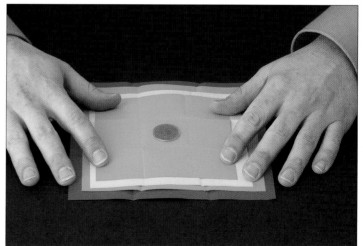

12 When you re-open the nest of papers the coin of high denomination will be revealed.

marked coin in ball of wool

A borrowed, marked coin vanishes, only to be discovered inside a small cloth bag in the centre of a ball of wool! This is a great trick – because it takes so long to reach the centre of the ball of wool, and the pouch is so well sealed up, it seems impossible that a borrowed coin could be inside. The preparation takes some time, so start getting it ready well in advance.

1 Take a piece of thick card (stock) about 10cm (4in) wide and 12cm (4¾in) long. Place a large coin in the middle of the card and mark its width on the card with a pencil. Draw straight lines this distance apart along the length of the card. Draw two more lines 3mm (⅛in) outside the existing lines.

2 Score along the marked lines and fold to create a long, flat tube. Use glue to stick the two sides together. Press together firmly between your thumb and fingers and allow it to dry completely before you release it.

3 When it is finished, the tube should be just big enough to allow a coin to slide along it with ease.

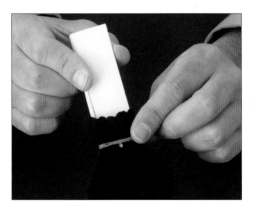

4 Insert one end of the coin slide into a small pouch and hold it in place with a tightly twisted rubber band around the neck of the pouch.

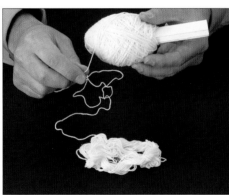

5 Wrap a ball of wool around the pouch and some of the cardboard tube.

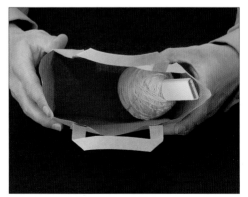

6 Place the finished article inside a paper bag, making sure that the coin slide faces upwards but cannot be seen.

7 To perform the trick, borrow a coin, have it marked with a pen and make it vanish using any of the methods explained in this book. Vanishing Coin in Handkerchief is ideal. Reach into the paper bag with the coin secreted in your right hand.

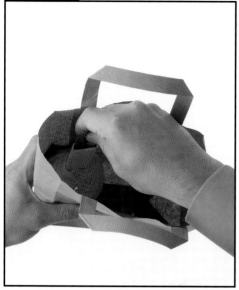

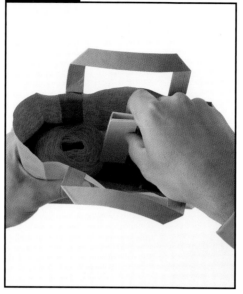

8 Secretly drop the coin into the prepared slide so that it is inserted in the bag in the centre of the ball of wool.

9 Pull the coin slide out of the ball of wool and leave it at the bottom of the bag as you take out the ball of wool. You may find you need to grip the wool through the bag with your left hand to assist in pulling out the slide.

10 Display the ball of wool to the spectators. Squeeze it slightly as you do so, to close-up the gap left by the coin slide.

11 Ask a volunteer from the audience to unwrap the ball of wool.

12 When they eventually finish unravelling the wool, which will take some time, they will discover the little pouch.

13 Ask them to verify that it is securely closed with the rubber band.

14 Ask them to open the pouch and remove the coin, and to verify that it is indeed the same coin that they marked earlier.

coin cascade

Ten coins are counted out loud and held by a spectator. Three invisible coins are tossed towards the spectator and when they open their hand and count the coins again they now have thirteen coins!

This is a great impromptu trick that can be performed almost anywhere. You can also substitute the coins for other small objects such as peanuts or sweets (candies).

1 You will need a hardback book and thirteen coins.

2 Insert three coins into the spine of the book. You will notice that when the book is closed the coins remain hidden and are held securely within the spine.

3 Display the remaining ten coins on the palm of your hand and hold the book in the other hand.

4 Give the coins in your hand to a volunteer. Open the book somewhere in the middle and ask the volunteer to count out loud as they place each of the coins on the book.

5 When they reach the last coin and say "ten", tip the coins into their cupped hands. The hidden coins will tip out with the other ten coins, completely unnoticed by your volunteer.

6 Mime throwing three invisible coins towards the volunteer, and ask them how many they would have if the coins were real. They will answer "thirteen".

7 Ask the person to count out the coins on to the book once again, and to their astonishment they will indeed have thirteen coins!

tip *A nice idea is to find a book on the subject of making money. Then when you do the trick you can mention that the information in the book works really fast!*

concorde coin (version 1)

In this simple yet incredibly effective trick, a coin is shown to have travelled invisibly from the right hand to the left. This is another of those rare tricks where the method is almost as impossible as the *effect. The coin really does travel invisibly from one hand to the other. For best results, perform the trick on a soft surface, such as a carpet or a tablecloth.*

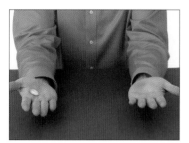   

1 Hold a small coin in the palm of your right hand. Notice how it is positioned, just below the base of the first and second fingers. Hold your left hand palm up as well, about 25cm (10in) from the right hand. The backs of your hands should be close to the floor or table.

2 Now turn both hands palm down very quickly. The right hand should move a fraction of a second before the left. With practice the coin will be flicked from the right hand to the left as they turn over. The coin moves so fast that the eye cannot see it. Fortunately, the camera can.

3 Take a few moments to explain that you are going to make the coin travel from your right hand to your left hand using magic. (Of course it is all done now, but as far as the spectators are concerned nothing has happened yet.)

4 Slowly raise your hands to show that the coin has indeed travelled across to the left hand. This really is a case of the hand being quicker than the eye.

concorde coin (version 2)

Here is an impressive variation of the trick above. Instead of using the surface of a table or the floor, this version can be performed *standing up. The moves are identical, apart from the fact that as the hands turn over they close into fists.*

1 Hold the coin in the palm of your right hand as before, and hold your left palm 25cm (10in) from your right hand.

2 Quickly flip your hands over, throwing the coin across to the left hand as you do so.

3 Having caught the coin, ball your hands into fists.

4 Open your hands to show the coin has travelled across.

tip *You can add a little misdirection to improve the trick still further. Start by showing the coin in your right hand then turn both hands over without throwing the coin. Say: "I am going to make the coin travel from my right hand to my left hand. In fact, it has already happened. But the hard thing is to make the coin travel back again … look, it's back." Open your hands and show the coin in your right hand where it has been all along. Of course this is a silly joke, but as soon as the spectators laugh you turn your hands over again (this time doing the secret move) and say: "No seriously, I can do it – watch." Performing it like this means that no one will see the move when you actually throw the coin because they think the trick is over. You do the move when they are least expecting it to happen.*

the coin test

While your back is turned, someone is asked to pick up a coin from the table and hold it high in the air in either hand. When they have lowered the hand, you turn around and are able to say with 100 per *cent accuracy which hand holds the coin. This clever mind-reading trick is a great impromptu stunt to remember the next time someone asks you to do something "off the cuff".*

1 Give someone a coin and ask them to place it in either hand while your back is turned. Then ask them to hold the coin high in the air and say: "Read my mind" five times.

2 When you compare their hands, one will be paler than the other. This is the one that holds the coin, since the blood will have left the hand while it was up in the air.

3 Finish by triumphantly pointing to the hand that holds the coin.

tip *To conceal your method you could start by asking the person to raise their right foot and then, say, look right and left before asking them to hold up the hand with the coin. People will think every move must have some meaning and therefore won't necessarily guess the true method.*

universal vanish

This simple sleight-of-hand trick is handy to know as you can make practically anything disappear with a wave of your hand. As with all *tricks, practice is essential to make it really work well. This works best if your spectators are seated opposite you.*

1 You need to be seated at a table. Have the object that is to vanish in front of you. In this case it is a coin.

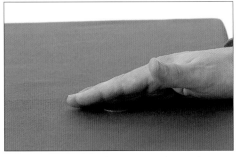

2 Turn your hand palm down so that it covers the coin and is almost flat on the table.

3 Move your hand forward until the coin touches the heel of your hand. Make small circular motions so the coin continues to slide beneath the heel of your hand.

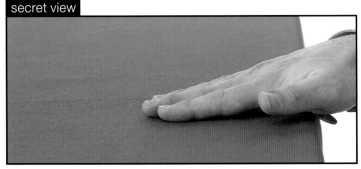

4 As the heel of your hand moves over the edge of the table the coin drops secretly into your lap.

5 The hand continues to "rub" the coin, moving forward and away from the table's edge. Finally, flip your hand over to show the coin has vanished.

gravity vanish

This technique is another great way to make many types of small objects seemingly disappear into thin air. Its success depends largely on timing and the use of angles. It must be seen just from the front, *so do not attempt to perform this trick if there is any possibility that the audience will have a view from the side, or you will give away the secret of how it is done.*

1 Hold a small object (in this case a coin) in your left hand. Notice how the object is held and displayed.

2 Rotate your hand at the wrist so that the back of your hand blocks the spectators' view of the coin.

3 Count to three, each time raising a finger. Notice how the right hand comes right in front of the left hand so that it is concealed from view.

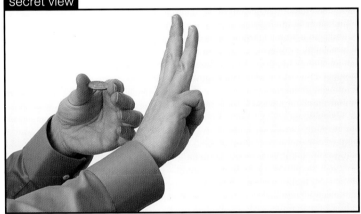

secret view

4 This view shows how things look from the side. The coin is hidden from the audience both by the angle at which it is being held and by the right hand.

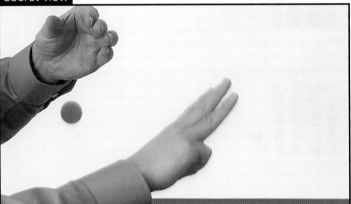

secret view

5 As you say "Three", drop your right hand to the table and simultaneously let the coin fall from your fingers. The left hand must not open its fingers but simply loosen its grip.

6 From the front, the coin's journey remains hidden behind your right hand.

7 Finish by rubbing your left fingers together and then opening the hand wide to show that the coin has gone.

unlinking safety pins

Two safety pins are clearly linked together but, amazingly, unlink three times in a row under challenge conditions. This little routine is an excellent one to learn as it can be performed impromptu or as part of a larger set, perhaps with some of the other safety pin tricks in this book, such as Pin-Credible and Safety Pin-a-tration. Although quite difficult to follow initially, once you have the knack it is simple.

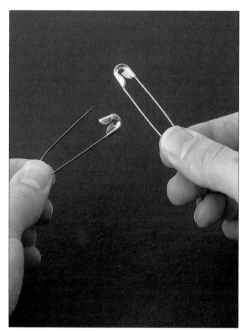

1 Hold one safety pin in your right hand and open the other. Notice how the open pin is oriented so that the head is to the right and open at the top. (For clarity, this pin has been coloured red.)

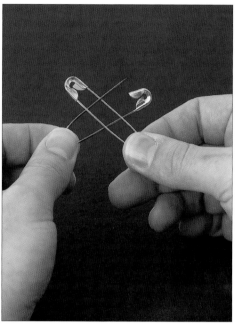

2 Thread this pin through the other. Make sure that the head of the pin in your left hand goes behind the other pin, while the open part goes through the middle. Close the pin.

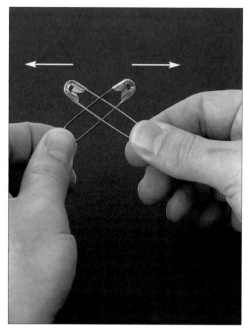

3 Now hold the pins by their ends and pull in opposite directions, as shown by the arrows.

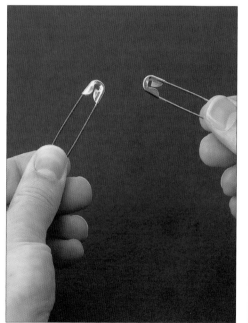

4 The spectator will be astonished that they come apart.

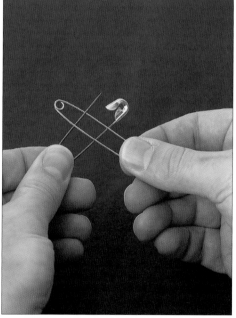

5 You can repeat this trick with a small change. Turn the pin in your right hand the other way up, as shown.

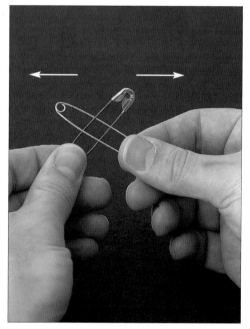

6 Link the pins in the same fashion as before and pull them apart.

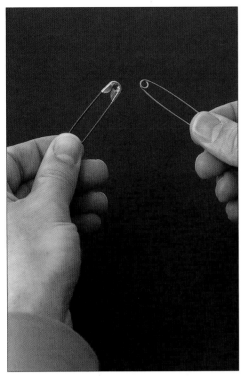

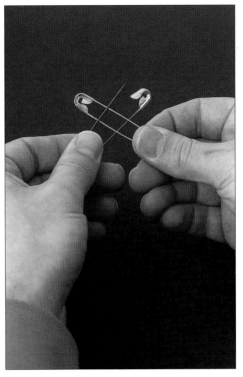

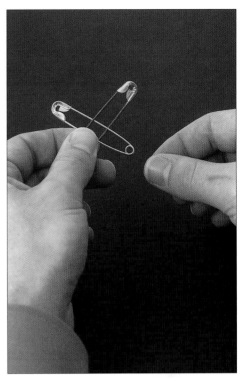

7 The safety pins will miraculously separate again! You can end the trick here, if you like, and hand out the safety pins for inspection, but it is a more impressive sequence if you continue and perform the grand finale.

8 For a finale, link the pins together one last time. However, as you can see, you don't actually link them together at all. The pin in your left hand goes over both sides of the other one, rather than going through the middle.

9 Pinch both pins between the tips your left thumb and fingers so that the pins stay together.

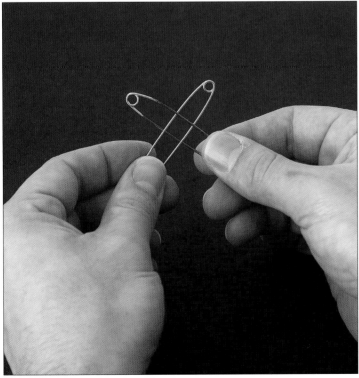

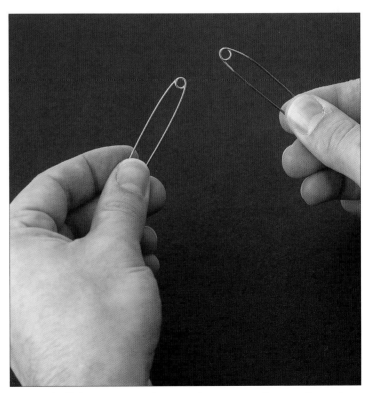

10 Turn the pins upside down, explaining that for the final time you will make the pins penetrate at the bottom instead of the top.

11 Pull them apart as the two pins apparently pass through one another one last time.

pin-credible

Five safety pins each have a different coloured bead attached. You turn your back on a volunteer and hold out your hands behind your back. The volunteer places one of the pins in your hand and hides the rest. You are magically able to divine which colour was chosen.

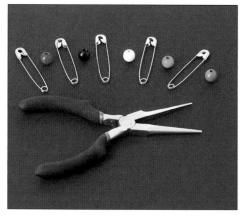

1 Find five beads of the same size but of different colours. You will also need five large safety pins and a pair of pliers.

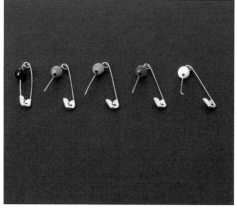

2 Open all five pins and thread on the five beads. Now you need to prepare each of the pins in a special way that you will be able to recognize.

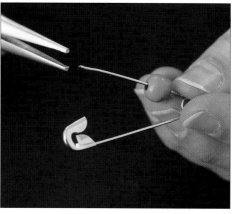

3 Clamp shut the head of the pin with the black bead, using the pliers.

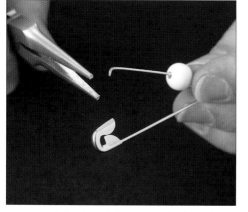

4 Bend the tip of the pin with the white bead threaded on to it.

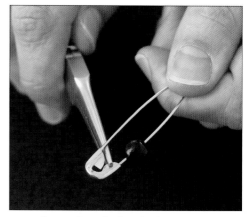

5 Bend the tip of the pin with the green bead in several places, to create a distinct surface.

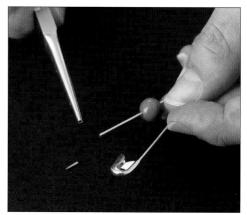

6 Cut off the tip of the pin with the blue bead. Each pin now looks the same when closed but, when opened, is distinct enough for you to feel which is which.

secret view

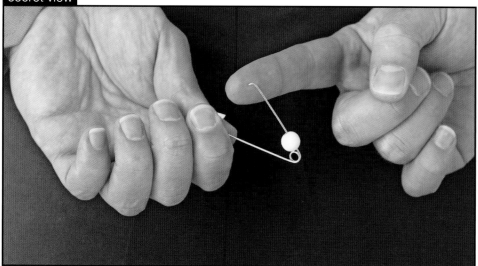

7 With the chosen pin behind your back, secretly open it as you turn to face the spectators again. Depending on what you can feel you now know which colour was chosen. Reveal it in a dramatic fashion and offer to repeat the trick.

safety pin-a-tration

A safety pin travels along the edge of a handkerchief before being removed without unfastening the pin. Practise this with an old *handkerchief until you understand the principles behind the trick. It will work consistently once you have mastered the moves.*

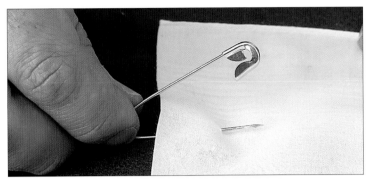

1 Secure a safety pin in the corner of a handkerchief, as shown in the picture above.

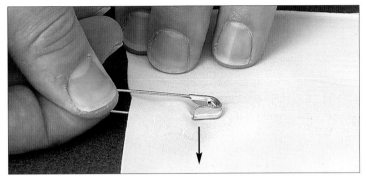

2 Hold the pin with the free top bar flat against the handkerchief, facing towards you. Slide the pin down to the far corner and the material will slip through the pin's fastener without damage. This is the first phase.

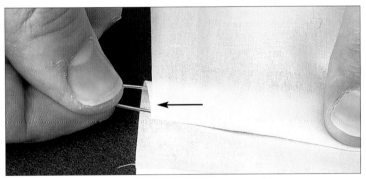

3 Turn the pin over three times, wrapping it in the cloth. Hold the cloth below the pin and pull it out with your right hand.

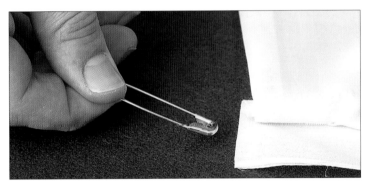

4 The safety pin will come free, still firmly closed, and the handkerchief will remain undamaged in every way.

domi-no-way

You show the audience that a prediction has been placed in a sealed envelope and set it to one side. Now you give two people a set of dominoes and tell them to arrange all the dominoes in any order they desire, ensuring that (just as in a proper game) each number matches *the number next to it. At the end you ask them to make a note of the two numbers at the end of the line of dominoes. When they open the envelope they discover, to their astonishment, that your prediction was correct; a baffling demonstration of your psychic abilities!*

1 The swindle is really very easy to carry out. Just remove one domino from a full set and make a note of the numbers. Then write this out as a prediction and seal it in an envelope.

2 Set the envelope on the table in full view and ask two people to set out the dominoes as described above.

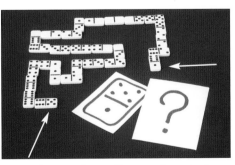

3 So long as they adhere to the rule that numbers next to each other must match they will always end up with the two numbers in your prediction at the ends of the line. Show that your prediction matches.

straw penetration

Two drinking straws are wrapped around one another and clearly tangled. Yet with a magical gesture the straws are pulled apart, *leaving both intact. We have used coloured straws in the photographs so that the moves are clear and easy to follow.*

1 Hold a drinking straw vertically in the fingertips of your left hand and another horizontally in the fingertips of your right hand. The horizontal straw is held in front of the vertical.

2 Wrap the bottom of the vertical straw up and away from you, around the horizontal straw.

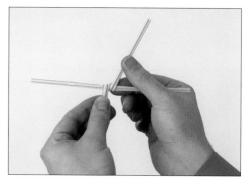

3 Continue wrapping it around the horizontal straw, bringing it back over until it is back where it started.

4 Now wrap the right end of the horizontal straw away from you and around the top half of the vertical straw, bringing it back to where it started.

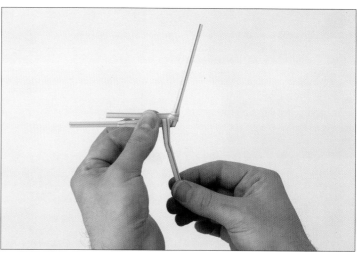

5 Wrap it back over one more time so that the two ends of the horizontal straw meet on the left.

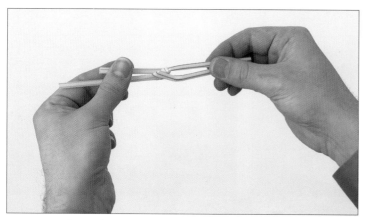

6 Bring the ends of the vertical straw together as well, and hold one straw in each hand.

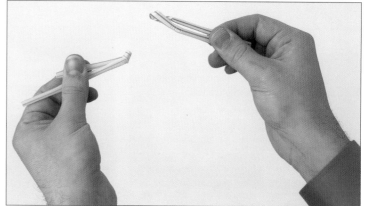

7 Pull your hands apart and incredibly the straws separate, seemingly penetrating each other. In fact the order and direction of the twists undo the previous twists, so while they look hooked together they are really not.

banana splitz

An unpeeled banana is magically cut into a number of pieces chosen by a spectator. Cards are used to make the trick more interactive and

allowing the spectator to choose how many times you slice the banana adds another layer of impossibility.

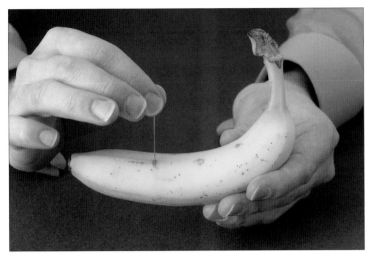

1 Prepare the banana by inserting a thin needle into the skin at three equally spaced intervals along its length and secretly slicing it by moving the needle in an arc. The banana should look quite normal when you have finished.

2 Place the banana on a plate in front of you and show five cards: an Ace, Two, Three, Four and Five of any suit. The Ace should be the top card.

3 Shuffle the cards, dragging one card off at a time, simply reversing the order. Then repeat, bringing the order of the cards back to how they were before you shuffled them. Now you need to make a spectator choose either the Three or the Four. Magicians call this a "force". Deal the cards face down and ask the person to say "Stop" at any time as you do so. Time things so that while you are telling them what to do, you deal past the first and second card. They will say "Stop" before the last card is dealt and therefore will stop you either at the Three or the Four.

4 If you are stopped at the Four, explain that you will magically chop the banana into four pieces. If you are stopped at the Three explain that you will make three magic karate chops. Mime three karate chops over the banana.

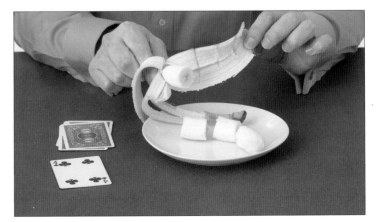

5 Peel the banana and allow the three or four pieces to fall on to the plate.

kiss me quick

A card is chosen by a spectator and shuffled back into the deck, which is then placed back in the box. The spectator blows a kiss at the deck of cards and when the cards are removed one card is seen reversed in the middle, with a big lipstick mark on its face. It is the chosen card.

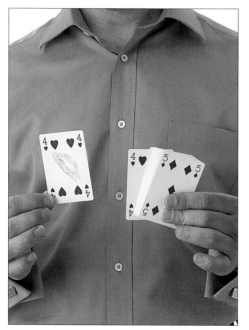

1 Prepare the trick by putting a lipstick kiss on the face of a card. You will need a duplicate of this card, which should be placed at the top of the deck.

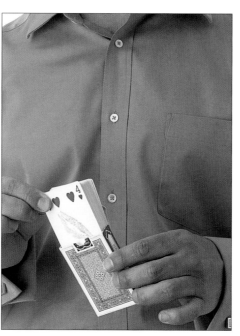

2 Place the deck in the box, with the "kiss" card at one end.

3 To perform the trick, remove the deck of cards from the box leaving the "kiss" card secretly within.

4 You will now force the duplicate card on to the spectator. (It should be the top face-down card.) Hold the deck on the palm of your hand and ask the spectator to cut a small number of cards off the deck and turn them face-up, returning them to the deck.

5 Now ask the spectator to cut a bigger batch of cards from the deck, turning those face-up too and replacing the pile once again.

6 Explain that the first face-down card you come to will be theirs. Spread through the deck and the very first face-down card will be your duplicate. (This technique is known to magicians as the "cut deeper force").

7 Ask your spectator to remember the card and then return it to the deck. Give the deck a shuffle.

8 Return the deck to the box. As you insert the cards be sure that the deck is oriented the opposite way around to the "kiss" card, which should be positioned somewhere in the middle of the deck.

9 Ask a female spectator who is wearing red lipstick to blow a kiss at the deck of cards.

10 Remove the deck from the box and spread out the cards face down. One card will be reversed and it will be the chosen card, with a great big kiss on it.

penetrating banknote

A folded banknote penetrates a strand of rubber band in a most visual way. This trick is similar to another trick called Bandit Bill, *although the method is slightly different. If you keep the prepared note with you at all times you can perform this trick at any time.*

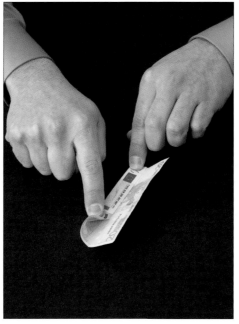

1 Prepare a banknote by carefully folding it in half along its length to make a sharp crease.

2 Unfold the note and then fold one half into the middle.

3 Repeat with the other side. The crease must be sharp for the trick to work.

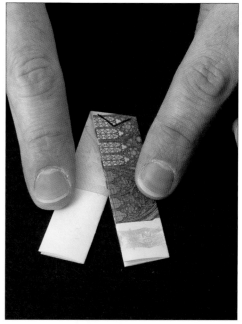

4 Refold the note along the first crease as shown.

5 Fold the banknote in half at an angle and crease it well so that it holds its shape after you let go.

6 Using a sharp craft knife cut a "V"-shaped notch near the fold, as shown. The cut should go through only one layer of the banknote. You are now ready to perform the trick.

7 Open the banknote and display it, holding it by your fingertips. You can use your index finger to hide the secret cut, although it is unlikely that anyone will see it. Refold the note.

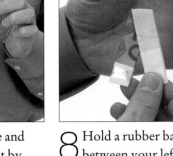

8 Hold a rubber band between your left thumb and first finger. Hold the folded banknote under the bottom strand of the band and make sure the "V" cut is at the back.

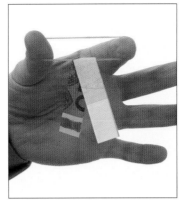

9 Raise the banknote to the band and allow the "V" to hook over the bottom strand. Let go and the banknote will hang as if it is actually folded over the band.

10 The illusion is perfect from the front but from the back you can see how the cut in the paper holds it against the band.

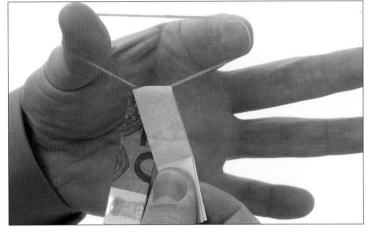

11 Gently pull the banknote downwards. This flexes the band and adds to the illusion greatly.

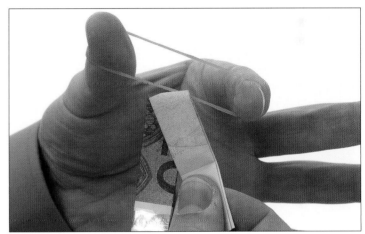

12 Slowly rub the banknote on the band and disengage the "V". Pull off the note very slowly and it will look as though it is melting through the rubber band.

13 Finally move the banknote away from the band and, if you wish, unfold it, smoothing down the "V" so that it can't be seen, and put it in your pocket.

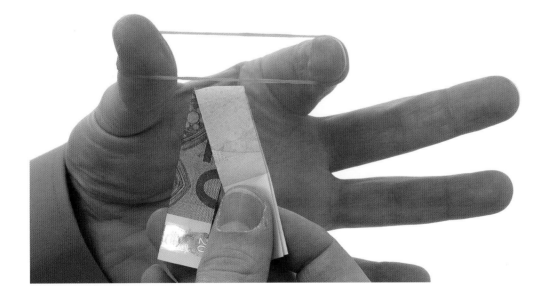

tip *You could keep a duplicate folded banknote in your pocket, so that if anyone asks to examine it closely you can remove the uncut note and show them.*

escaping jack

You display a card with a hole punched through its centre, along with a small envelope with a matching hole. You place the card inside and secure it with a ribbon running through all the holes. Despite being secured with the ribbon, the card is pulled free and proves to be completely unscathed. If you like you could substitute the card with a cut out figure of Harry Houdini to add an extra element to the trick.

1 You will need an old playing card, a hole punch, a 50cm (20in) length of thin ribbon, a pair of scissors and an envelope that is just larger than the card.

2 Prepare the envelope by cutting a tiny sliver off the bottom so that the envelope is bottomless.

3 Punch a small hole in the centre of the envelope.

4 Punch or cut a small hole, using scissors or a knife, exactly in the centre of the playing card.

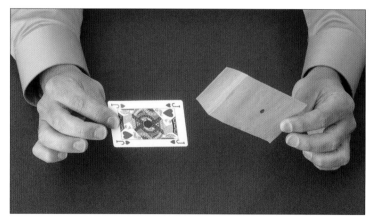

5 Show both sides of the card and the envelope to the spectators and slowly insert the card into the envelope until it is completely inside.

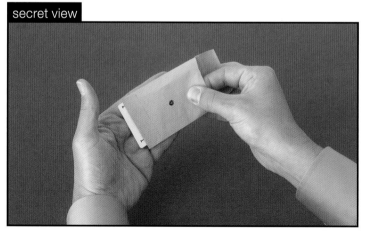

secret view

6 Give the playing card an extra push so that it starts to emerge from the bottom of the envelope, as shown. The left hand hides this from the front.

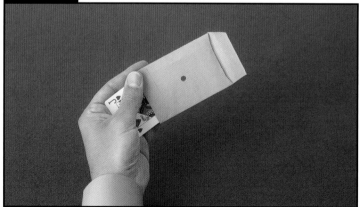

secret view

7 The card needs to be pulled out far enough to clear the hole in the centre of the envelope.

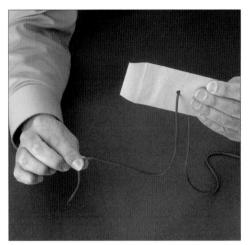

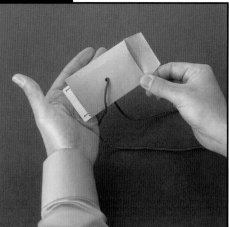

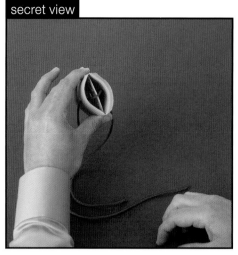

8 From the front everything looks as it should. Thread the ribbon through the holes in both sides of the envelope.

9 As soon as the ribbon is through the hole, push the card completely back into the envelope.

10 This view inside the envelope shows how the ribbon runs over the top of the card.

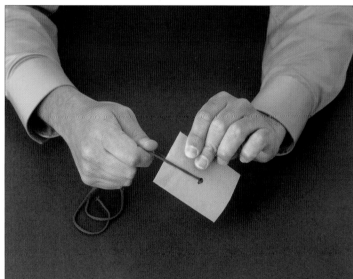

11 Seal the envelope and show both sides to the spectators so that they can see that the ribbon goes through it.

12 Grasp the envelope firmly in one hand and both ends of the ribbon in the other.

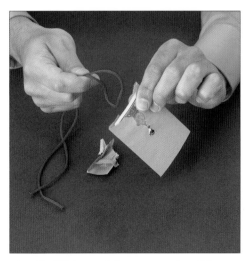

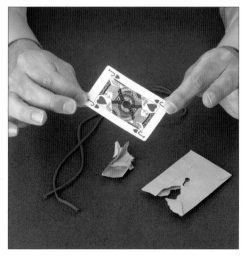

13 With a quick tug, tear the ribbon through the envelope.

14 Remove the card and show that it is totally unharmed.

tip *You will need to rehearse this trick several times before you attempt to perform it to an audience. It would be a good idea to prepare a number of envelopes at the same time as you can use each one only once.*

card on wall

There is a classic magic trick called Card on Ceiling, in which a chosen, signed card is shuffled into a deck. The deck is thrown in the air and the signed card flies out of the pack and sticks to the ceiling.

The problem with this is that it can be difficult to get the card down again and some people object to having a card stuck on their ceiling long after the show is over. So here is a simplified method that looks just as good, which you will be able to use in any venue without

ruining the décor. Instead of using the ceiling you stick the card on to a wall or a glass picture frame.

On the other hand, if you have permission or it is your house, you may choose to stick the card to the ceiling. If you throw the card somewhere that can't be reached the result of your trick will last long after you have left. There will be a story to tell every time someone asks, "Why is there a card stuck to the ceiling?".

1 You will need a deck of cards and a piece of adhesive tape. Make the tape into a loop with the sticky side out. The loop should fit loosely around the middle finger of your right hand.

2 Spread a deck of cards in a fan, for a selection to be made.

secret view

3 Take care to keep the tape away from the deck.

4 Ask someone to select a card and remember what it is.

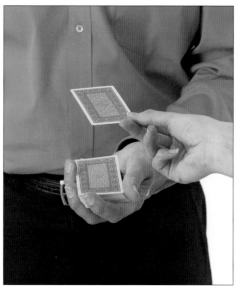

5 Ask them to replace their card on the top of the deck.

secret view

6 Turn the deck over and secretly allow the tape to stick to the back of their card. Slip the loop of tape off your finger.

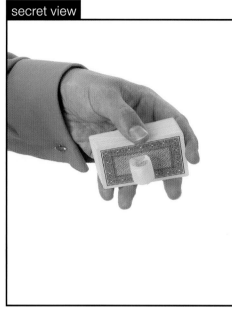

7 Prepare to shuffle the deck of cards. Be sure to keep the tape out of the spectators' view.

8 Notice how this overhand shuffle keeps the chosen card in place at the back of the deck. Squeeze the front and back cards every time you take a batch and the chosen card never moves. From the front this looks like a genuine shuffle.

9 Prepare to "spring" the cards from your hand by bending them as shown, but don't let the audience see the tape. Aim the cards with the tape pointing directly at the wall.

11 The chosen card remains stuck to the wall for a spectacular finish.

tip *You will probably want to use an old deck of cards for this trick, as the cards will end up all over the floor. Try not to let anyone else remove the card from the surface, or they will see how it is stuck: remove it yourself after the show.*

10 Spring the cards at the wall and the selection will stick firmly while all the other cards cascade to the floor.

spooky matchbox

A matchbox on the back of your hand stands up and lies back down all on its own. Although this is one of the first tricks most magicians ever learn, very few realize just how good it looks. Try it, practise it and you will have another great trick to perform with no extra props beyond the matchbox. As you gain skill you can make the box stand and lie down with minimal movement and under your control.

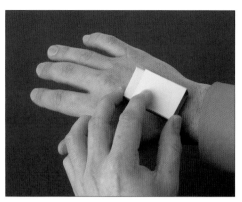

1 Remove the cover of a matchbox and replace it upside down.

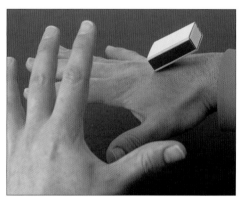

2 Hold out your right hand, palm down, and put the matchbox (partially opened) on the back of your hand. The open part of the box should be just behind your knuckles.

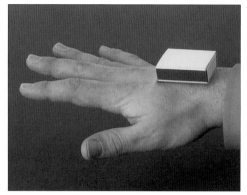

3 Now shut the matchbox, pushing down as you close it and trapping a small piece of your skin in the drawer. This looks painful but does not hurt at all. You may need to arch your fingers upward to facilitate the action. At the very least the fingers should be absolutely straight when you do this.

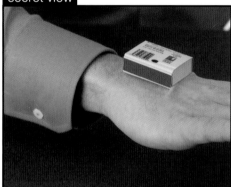

secret view

4 The view from this side clearly shows the flap of skin trapped in the drawer of the box.

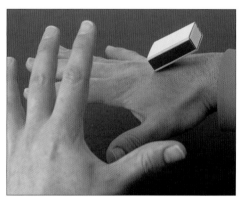

5 By stretching open your fingers and flexing them as far apart as possible you will stretch the skin and the box will slowly stand up on its own.

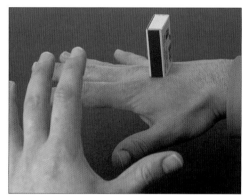

6 Make a mystical pass with your left hand as it stands up, to add some misdirection and mystery.

7 By closing your hand into a fist you will disengage the trapped skin from the box.

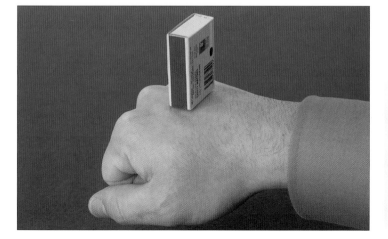

tip *The trick looks much better when you turn your hand so that the box is viewed from the end opposite the trapped skin. Remember this when showing it to others.*

swapping checkers

On the table are a column of white checkers and a column of brown checkers. Each column is covered with a paper tube and the two are moved around so that no one knows which colour is under which tube.

A spectator makes a guess and the magician shows everyone whether they were correct. Regardless, with a magical wave the two piles change places instantaneously.

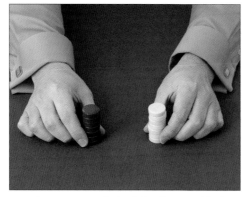

1 You will need seven brown checkers, seven white checkers and two sheets of paper. Paint the bottom of one brown checker white and the bottom of one white checker brown.

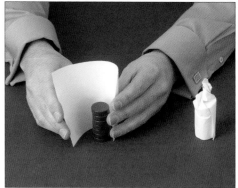

2 Create two piles of checkers, with the double-sided checker on the bottom of each pile.

Use a piece of paper to wrap each column of checkers. The paper should not be too tight.

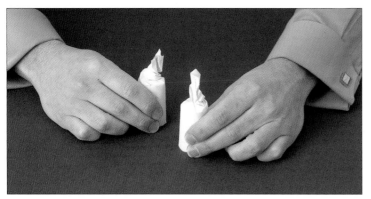

4 Move the two columns around, sliding the two paper tubes on the surface of the table. Explain that if you don't watch closely it is difficult to know where each colour is. Ask someone to guess where the brown pile is.

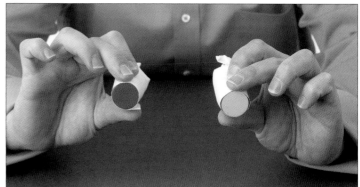

5 Whichever pile they point to tilt both backwards and show the colours. Of course, what they actually see is the painted undersides of the prepared checkers.

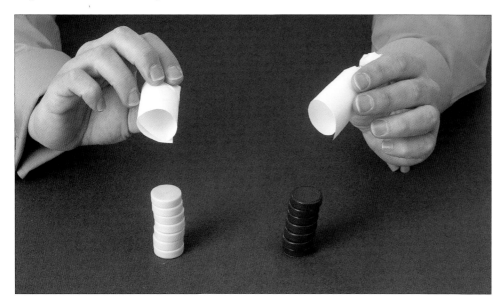

6 Make a magical gesture as you say that you are going to make the two columns of checkers change places. Lift the paper tube off each pile to show that this has happened.

tip *For an even better effect, scan one of each colour of checker on a computer, print them out at life size in colour, then cut around them and stick them to the bottom of the checkers.*

indestructible string

A length of string is wrapped in a piece of paper. The paper is clearly cut into two pieces and yet the string is somehow completely unharmed. "Cut and Restored" is a classic theme in magic; the impossibility of tearing, cutting or sawing something or someone in two and restoring it or them has fascinated audiences worldwide for hundreds of years.

1 You will need a piece of string approximately 50cm (20in) long, a pair of scissors and a piece of paper about 10 x 7.5cm (4 x 3in).

2 Make a fold about 2.5cm (1in) up from the bottom of the paper. Now fold the top piece down so that it just overlaps the bottom edge of the paper. This completes the preparation.

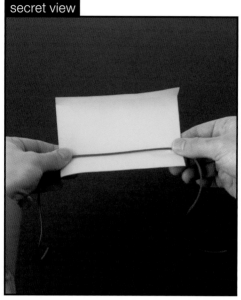

3 To perform the trick, hold the folded paper open, towards you, and lay the string along the lower crease. Notice how the thumbs of each hand pinch the string and paper to hold it all in place.

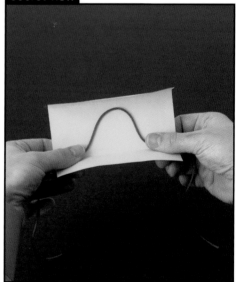

4 Now lift the bottom flap of the paper upwards, towards you, with your middle fingers and at the same time slide your thumbs inwards so that the middle of the string becomes a loop.

5 This action is completely unseen from the front.

6 Continue to fold up the flap and grip the string through the paper with your thumbs, as shown here.

secret view

7 Keeping your thumbs still, use your left index finger to pull the loop of string down.

secret view

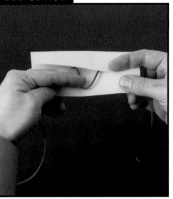

8 Now fold over the top flap of the paper using your right forefinger.

secret view

9 Grip the paper and string with your left hand as shown. Pinch the loop of string inside the paper with your thumb to make sure it stays still. Remove your right hand.

secret view

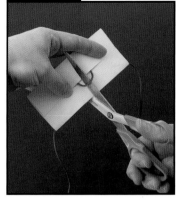

10 As you prepare to cut the paper, insert the top blade of the scissors through the loop and adjust the position of your grip so your fingers straddle the blades and hold on to both sides of the paper. Mind your fingers!

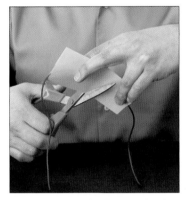

11 From the front it looks as though you are going to cut through both the paper and the string.

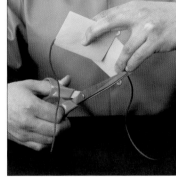

12 With one snip, cut the paper in two. Ensure that the half of the paper in front overlaps the half at the back to hide the intact string and maintain the illusion.

13 Slide the two pieces of paper apart, showing the string intact in the middle.

tip *If you are left handed, simply reverse the hand positions so that you can cut using your left hand.*

magnetic cards

Rubbing your hand on your sleeve to generate static, you proceed to stick over a dozen playing cards to your palm-down, outstretched hand. This trick may require a bit of practice in order to perfect it, *but once you get used to how the cards are positioned you will find it an easy matter to succeed every time. There are many different ways of performing this famous and popular trick.*

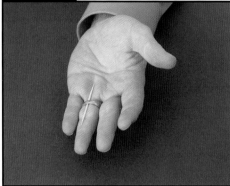

secret view

1 You will need to be wearing a ring for this trick. Place a toothpick under the ring and keep it hidden as you rub your hand on your sleeve, supposedly to generate static.

2 Hold your hand flat on the table and take the first card, placing it sideways in between the toothpick and your fingers.

3 Now add two more cards, as shown, sliding them between the first card and your fingers.

secret view

4 This view from underneath shows the configuration of the first three cards.

5 Carefully add more and more cards, making a haphazard petal-like pattern, until about twelve cards have been used.

6 Finally, slowly lift your hand into the air and all the cards will cling to your palm as if magnetized!

secret view

7 The secret view shows how the cards remain trapped by the toothpick against the palm of your hand.

8 Place your hand back on the table and use your other hand to separate the cards, disengaging the toothpick and leaving the normal cards to be examined by your now amazed spectators.

picture perfect

A sheet of paper is torn into nine pieces. Eight pieces are left blank and a spectator draws a simple picture on the ninth. The magician is blindfolded and by touch alone – apparently from psychic vibes – is able to find the piece of paper with the picture on it. To finish, the magician makes a quick sketch, still blindfolded, and the picture matches that drawn by the spectator.

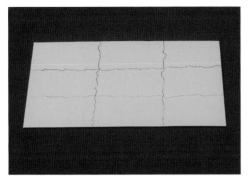

1 Tear a sheet of thin card (stock) or paper into nine pieces along the lines shown here.

2 Ensure that the tears are not too neat – they should be as rough as possible.

3 Notice that the central piece of card or paper is the only one that has four torn sides. This is the key to this trick. Hand out this piece of card or paper and ask someone to draw a simple picture on it, keeping it hidden from you.

4 Meanwhile, blindfold yourself using a handkerchief.

secret view

5 After the spectator has drawn the picture, ask them to mix all the papers together and then to hand them to you behind your back. Take each piece of paper in turn and feel the edges to determine which piece has four torn sides. This is the one with the picture on it. Bring it to the front and show that you found it.

6 If you are blindfolded with a handkerchief you will find that you can still see down the side of your nose, even if the blindfold is quite tight. Glance at the picture when you bring it to the front.

7 Make a quick sketch of the same subject while you are still blindfolded.

8 Finish by removing your blindfold and revealing that the pictures match!

beads of mystery

Three beads magically escape from two pieces of cord on to which they are tied. This trick is interesting as the method can be adapted *for all kinds of tricks, large and small. You will find other tricks in this book that use a similar principle.*

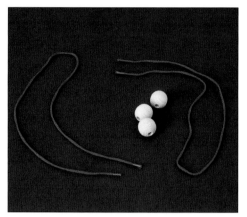

1 You will need three large beads and two pieces of thin cord, each approximately 30cm (12in) long.

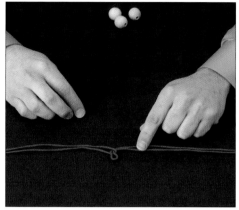

2 Prepare by folding both cords in half and then looping the centre of one through the other.

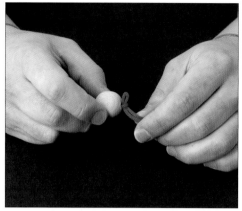

3 Thread a bead on to the right-hand cord and slip the looped centres inside the bead so that the preparation is hidden.

4 Thread the other two beads on to the cords, one on each side. From all angles it looks as though you have three beads threaded on two lengths of cord. Only you know that the cords are looped.

5 Display the beads on the cord to your audience and explain that you are tying a knot to make sure they are secure.

6 Hold the cords at either end and place the beads on the palm of a spectator's outstretched hand.

7 Ask the spectator to close their hand tightly over the beads.

8 Pull on the cords and the beads will be released into the spectator's hand.

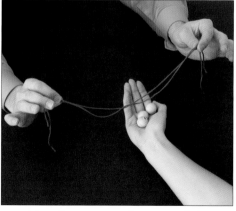

9 After the spectator has opened their hand you can give everything out for closer examination.

sweet tooth

A small paper bowl is shown to contain four candies. It is covered with a second bowl and shaken. The candies are shown to have somehow multiplied so that now there are seven. When the bowls are shaken once again only four remain.

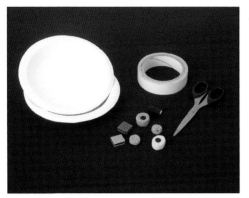

1 You will need two paper bowls, some double-sided adhesive tape, seven candies and a pair of scissors.

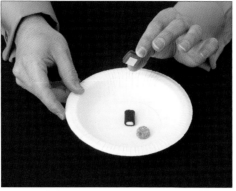

2 To prepare the trick, cut three small pieces of tape and stick three candies to the base of one of the bowls.

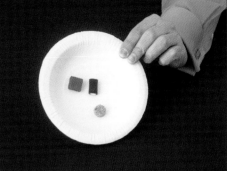

3 The positioning of these candies should look random.

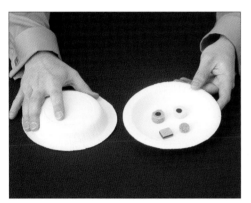

4 In performance, hide the three taped candies by holding that bowl upside down on a surface. Show the other bowl, which contains four loose candies, to the spectators.

5 Cover the bowl containing the loose candies with the inverted bowl.

6 Now turn the bowls over three or five times. As you do so, the candies will rattle inside for all to hear. Because you have turned the bowls an odd number of times the bowl with the fixed candies will now be at the bottom.

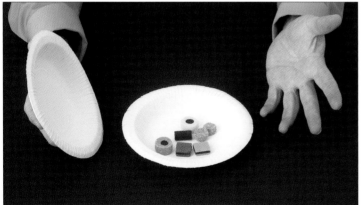

7 Lift the top bowl, showing it to be empty and at the same time asking someone to count how many candies are in the bowl now. Of course there will be three more than before, as the ones that are glued to the base are now included in the count.

8 Finish by either nesting the empty bowl under the other one and removing and eating a candy, or placing the empty bowl over the one containing the candies, and turning the bowl an odd number of times so that the bowl with fixed candies is at the top. When you lift it off, only the four loose candies will be visible.

ping-pong balance

A piece of rope and a ping-pong ball are shown to the spectators. The ball is then magically balanced on the rope and even made to roll backwards and forwards without falling. Defying gravity is a favourite theme for magicians, and is used in almost all types of magic. If you can perform this smoothly, it is almost as if the ball is under your complete control.

1 Prepare a piece of rope by stitching a length of fine thread of a similar colour to it at both ends.

2 Place the ping-pong ball on a stand made from a rolled-up piece of card (stock). Stretch the rope out between your hands. The rope and thread should be held as in the previous picture.

3 Lower the rope so that it goes in front of the ball while the thread goes behind it.

4 Slowly lift the rope and the ball will look as though it is balanced on it.

5 Tilt the rope gently to one side and the ball will roll along it without falling off.

6 Slowly lower your hands to return the ball to its stand and release the ends of the rope.

zero gravity

The mouth of a bottle of water is covered with a small piece of paper and inverted. The water remains inside the bottle. The paper is removed but the water still defies gravity. Finally, toothpicks are fed into the neck of the bottle, proving there is nothing to stop the water from gushing out. This trick takes practice to execute confidently and it's a good idea to practise over a sink.

1 You will need to make a special gimmick: a disc of clear plastic just a fraction larger than the mouth of the bottle you are using.

2 Punch a hole in the middle of the plastic and the gimmick is ready.

3 Take a small square of paper and dip it into a glass of water to wet it.

secret view

4 You must secretly hold the plastic disc under this piece of paper.

5 Place the wet plastic disc and paper against the mouth of the bottle and hold it tightly as you turn the bottle upside down.

6 Very carefully let go and you will find the paper and water remain suspended. Now remove the paper, leaving the disc in place.

secret view

7 This close-up view shows how the gimmick keeps the water in.

8 Insert a toothpick into the hole in the disc.

9 Watch as the toothpick floats to the surface of the water. This sight is incredible and it looks like real magic.

10 Finally, turn the bottle upright again.

11 As you do so, secretly remove the gimmick from the mouth of the bottle and hide it in your hand.

tip *This trick can be done close-up with care, as the disc is invisible at very close quarters. If you want extra reliability you can purchase a relatively cheap gimmick from a magic shop.*

take cover

A matchbox is shaken and heard to contain matches. The box is opened and the matches are definitely there, but the matchbox cover vanishes into thin air! It reappears inside the magician's pocket. This clever prop should only take about 10 minutes to construct.

1 You will require two matchboxes, some glue and a pair of scissors to make this trick.

2 First separate the cover and the drawer of one matchbox. Cut the side and front off the cover.

3 Glue this to the base and side of the drawer, as marked in the picture.

4 Make sure the edges do not overlap by trimming any excess card away. Remove and discard the drawer from the other matchbox, and put the cover in your pocket. Put some matches in the prepared drawer and you are ready to perform the trick.

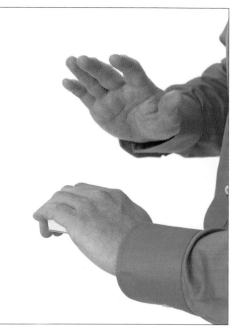

5 To perform, hold the fake matchbox upside down so that the top and side face the audience. The matches will be loose so be careful they don't fall out of the inverted box. Shake the box and say: "Watch carefully."

6 Close your fingers around the box and turn your hand over. You must now turn your body so your left side is facing the spectators.

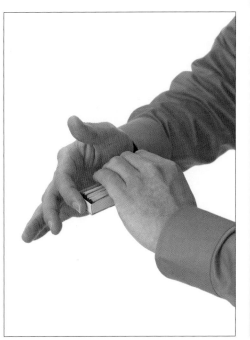

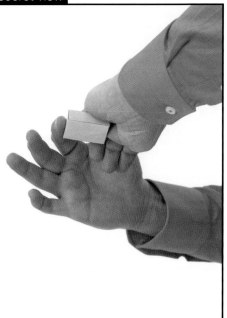

7 Use your left thumb to push the drawer out from your hand and take it with your right hand. The illusion is perfect. The gimmicked top and side will be hidden.

8 This is the view of how the box is held from beneath.

9 Wait a few seconds in the position shown. Your friends will believe you have the match box cover in your left hand.

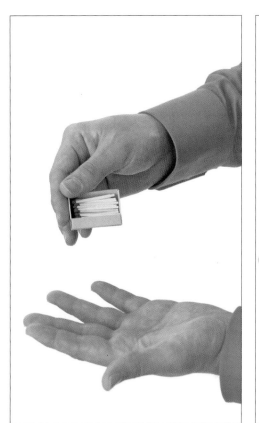

10 Crumple the fingers of your left hand and open them to show that the box has gone.

11 Transfer the drawer to your left hand, and reach into your pocket with your right hand to remove the duplicate cover.

12 Slide the duplicate cover over your gimmicked box to finish the trick.

enchanted ball

A golf ball is placed on a table and with the apparent use of telekinetic powers is caused to move all on its own. This trick takes *a lot of careful preparation but would work really well if you have friends over for dinner and rig the table before they arrive.*

1 You will need a golf ball, a key ring, a needle, some fishing line and a small bead. A large bead and bright thread have been used here for clarity, but you should use thin fishing line and a small bead.

2 Attach a long length of fishing line to the key ring. Set this on a table and run the line off the far end.

secret view

3 Cover with a tablecloth and run the line under the table and back to your side. Using a needle, thread the line through the tablecloth and secure the end of the thread to a small bead.

secret view

4 Show a golf ball to the spectators, handing it out for examination. Take back the ball and put it on the table, on top of the key ring, which should be invisible under the tablecloth. Engage the bead in between your fingers and strike a pose.

5 Wave your hands over the ball and slowly move them backwards. The ball will start to move away from you. When it reaches the far side lift it up in the air and toss it out to be examined as you covertly drop the bead behind the table.

what a mug!

This is a very easy and fun practical joke to play on your friends, and requires just a coin and a mug. Although this trick is a simple "gag", *it is the perfect prelude to Mugged Again and will add an element of humour to the routine.*

1 Place a coin on a table and cover it with a mug. Tell the spectators that it is possible for you to pick up the coin without even touching the mug. When they say they don't believe you, ask them if they want to make a small bet.

2 Say, "It's easy because I never really put the coin under the mug in the first place." When someone lifts the mug to check if it's still there, simply pick up the coin from the table and demand your winnings.

mugged again!

This is a perfect follow-up trick to What a Mug! This time you tell the spectators that you will get a from coin under a mug while they hold the mug pinned to the table. You will need to use a little sleight-of-hand but it is not too difficult.

secret view

1 Hold a coin secretly in the fingers of your right hand. Show a similar coin at your fingertips and place it on the table, then cover it with a mug.

secret view

2 Explain and demonstrate that you are going to get a coin under the mug while they hold their finger on the top of the mug. Keep the other coin secreted in your right hand. This is a view from your angle.

3 From the front the coin remains hidden and your right hand looks relaxed and normal.

secret view

4 Now comes the fun part. Tilt the mug away from you and reach inside as if you are removing the coin from the table. Actually you leave the coin where it is and push the hidden coin to your fingertips under the mug. It is the hidden coin that you bring into view.

5 From the front it looks just as though you have removed the coin.

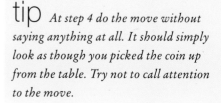

6 Now a spectator pins the mug to the table with their finger and you ask them to close their eyes so they can't see how it is done. When their eyes are closed tap the coin in your hand against the mug to make it sound as if you are doing something, then put the coin in your pocket.

7 Tell the spectator to open their eyes and have a look under the mug – the coin will still be there!

tip *At step 4 do the move without saying anything at all. It should simply look as though you picked the coin up from the table. Try not to call attention to the move.*

party
tricks

Every party you attend will be that much more exciting once you know how to perform a few simple party tricks. Some are amazing demonstrations of strength, speed and mental agility, while others are designed to create laughter, amusement and amazement. Many of these party tricks can be incorporated into your magic show to enliven your presentations and get the audience involved.

introduction

Nowadays there are so many new tricks flooding on to the market all the time that most magic shops and suppliers tend to list their wares in on-line catalogues, which are widely accessible and can be easily and quickly updated. However, in the "olden days" almost all magic shops used to design and produce beautifully bound publications that were full of detailed descriptions and advertisements for their stock. In an attempt to promote their latest lines and appeal to as many customers as possible, the advertisements in the old magic catalogues would often promise that if you just learnt *this one trick* you would become the life and soul of your next party. Many of these older catalogues have now become collectors' items.

While one party trick, however impressive, may not be enough to form the basis of a prolonged performance, a few fun items that you can casually introduce in a party-like atmosphere can certainly add some memorable moments to an otherwise ordinary social event. Although the average party trick may not create such a sense of mystery and wonder in your audience as a good magic trick, or result in the satisfaction you would derive from that kind of performance, the tricks and jokes assembled in this chapter can be great fun to perform in a more relaxed and informal situation.

Party tricks are generally simple to do and don't need much in the way of props or preparation. These off-the-cuff demonstrations often use objects that just happen to be close by, and once you have learnt a few of the tricks described here you will be able

Above: A typical magic shop. The display window is crammed full of magic props, practical jokes and exciting things to look at. Magic shops often stock fancy dress goods and other novelty items too.

to prepare something quickly and easily using the resources around you. Party tricks are also an ideal way to entertain young children, and in several cases (such as Jacob's Ladder and Jacob's Tree) the children can even help to make the tricks happen.

Looking at the bigger picture, some of these party tricks can be incorporated into a routine with other magic tricks. For instance, if you are planning to perform Vanishing Coin in Handkerchief, you can incorporate a simple sight gag using the same prop, such as Obedient Handkerchief or Milo the Mouse, as a prelude to the trick. By adding party tricks to your magic repertoire you can begin to build routines that make for a more rounded performance.

Here is another example of how a party trick can be incorporated into the performance of a magic trick or illusion. The picture opposite shows a standard performance of the illusion known as Sword

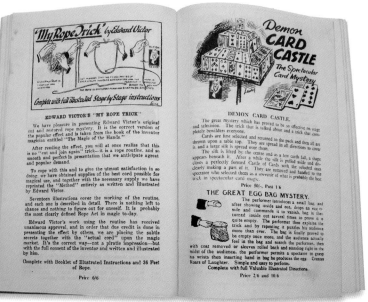

Left: A 1950's Davenports' magic catalogue reveals how to do some simple and well-loved tricks, the props for which would have been available in-store. L. Davenports & Co have been makers of magic since 1898.

Above: British comedy legend Tommy Cooper (1922–84). Cooper became famous for his tricks going wrong. It was this failure to perform the magic tricks correctly that formed the basis of many of his comedy routines.

The British comedy legend Tommy Cooper (1922–84) was also a successful practitioner of this type of party trick. His deliberate blunders used to delight audiences, who would holler with laughter as he stumbled through trick after trick. Although he rarely performs magic today, USA's Tom Mullica is one of the funniest magicians around. His sleight-of-hand and repertoire of fine magic is complemented by and interspersed with his crazy moments of comedy, and this combination takes his act from exceptionally baffling to completely awesome.

Once you have experimented with the collection of party tricks in this chapter you may find that you can get the best reactions when you perform them without calling attention to them. For instance, Loose Thread, in which someone who thinks they are removing a piece of thread from your clothing finds that they are apparently unravelling all the stitching in your shirt, wouldn't be nearly as funny if you pointed out the loose end of the thread and asked them to remove it. The best reactions occur when you are having a conversation with a friend and they think they are being helpful trying to smarten up your shirt or jacket. Use these party tricks in the right situation and at the right time and you will receive a tremendous amount of satisfaction from the fun and laughter you will generate.

Suspension. The magician's assistant appears to be supported on the tip of a sword, and it is very impressive to look at as it is. But this idea has been further developed by the German sensation Hans Moretti. He makes two "beanstalks" or Jacob's Trees from newspapers in front of his audience and uses them in place of the standard swords when suspending his assistant. This takes the trick to a new height. It is a creative, exciting and original way of presenting what might otherwise seem a tired and over-used illusion, and links two tricks together in a smooth way.

There are many magicians who are known for incorporating such party tricks or "bits of business" around the magic in their acts. Most of them are performers who rely on comedy and humour. One such performer was Bob Read (1940–2005), a British magician who provided as much entertainment with his party tricks as he did with his excellent magic. He performed the Obedient Handkerchief better than anyone and could get a full five minutes of comedy from this one party trick alone.

Below: A magician, Gogia Pasha, defies the laws of gravity by suspending his assistant on the tip of a sharp sword in 1959. The spectators standing behind the performers are clearly startled and baffled by what they see, since there is no visible sign of how she is being supported.

Jasper the ghost

This very simple and strange party trick will leave someone wondering if ghosts really do exist, after they feel a tap on their *shoulder while no one else is around. For reasons that will become obvious, this trick works best one-on-one.*

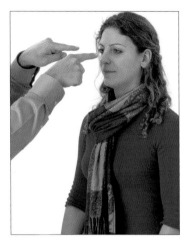

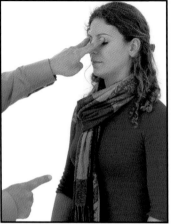
secret view

secret view

1 Tell the person that you know a friendly ghost who would like to meet them. Hold the first finger of each hand about 10cm (4in) away from their eyes, then ask them to close their eyes.

2 As soon as their eyes close, move your right hand away and spread the first and second fingers of your left hand as shown. Lightly touch their eyelids with these two fingers. They will feel the sensation of a finger on each eyelid and will assume that both your hands are occupied.

3 Call out for your ghost friend "Jasper" and tap the person on the shoulder with your free hand.

4 Immediately bring your hands back to the original position and when the person opens their eyes everything will look as it did before.

trip to China

Next time you have to serve a cup of tea try this out and you'll make your friends jump for sure. But don't try it if someone is already *holding a hot drink, as they will spill it. Always be sensible when you try a practical joke of this type.*

secret view

1 Hold an empty teacup and saucer in your right hand. You will also need a teaspoon.

2 Put the spoon handle through the handle of the cup. Grip the spoon handle firmly between your thumb and the saucer.

3 Approach someone as if you were going to offer them a cup of hot tea. Grip the saucer and spoon tightly and pretend to trip. The cup will fall forward and make a big noise, but it won't fall as it will be trapped by the bowl of the spoon.

removal man

After a bottle of wine has been finished, push the cork right into the bottle. The challenge is to remove the cork without breaking either the cork or the bottle. It seems an impossible task, but it is actually quite easy when you know the secret of how it is done.

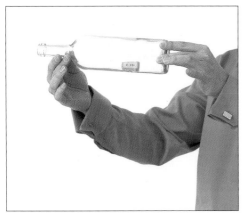

1 When you have finished a bottle of wine, rinse it out, dry it and then push the cork into the empty bottle.

2 Twist a table napkin until it is rope-like and insert it into the neck of the bottle. Keep pushing the napkin in until it is as far down as you can get it.

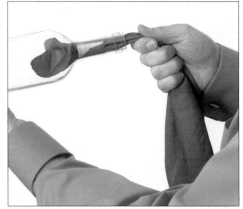

3 Turn the bottle upside down and shake it until the cork is caught up in the folds. You may need to try several times until the cork is upright rather than side-on. Slowly pull out the napkin; the cork will remain trapped within the folds.

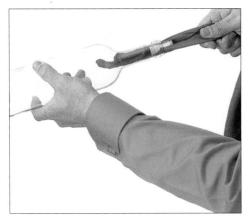

4 Continue to pull until the cork comes out of the bottle.

5 Show your audience what you have achieved and take a bow!

tip *As with most tricks in this book, the more you practise this trick the easier it becomes to do well. So don't be disheartened if you find it difficult initially – it will get easier and you will soon be able to perform with ease.*

saucy beggar

This is a really good practical joke, perfect for when you're enjoying a meal with friends. If you don't want to go to the trouble of making this prop yourself at home, there are often ready made ones available in magic stores or on the internet.

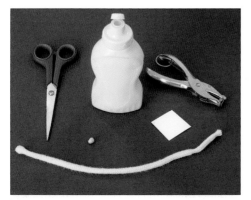

1 You will need an empty squeezable mustard bottle, some thick yellow cord (the cord in these pictures was coloured with food dye), reusable putty adhesive, a small piece of card (stock), a hole punch and a pair of scissors.

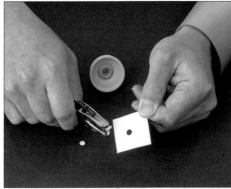

2 Open the lid of the empty bottle by unscrewing it and thoroughly clean and dry the lid and bottle. Punch a hole in the piece of card.

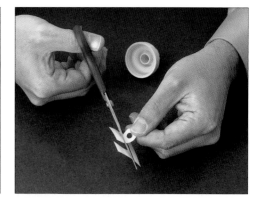

3 Trim the card around the hole to make a collar that will sit neatly inside the lid of the bottle.

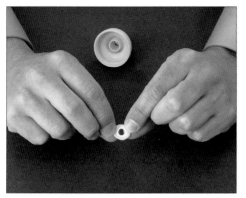

4 Use reusable putty adhesive to stick the collar to the inside of the lid.

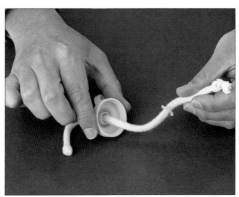

5 Before sticking the collar into place, thread the length of yellow cord through the hole in the lid and through the collar. Tie a knot in the end, which will eventually sit in the bottle.

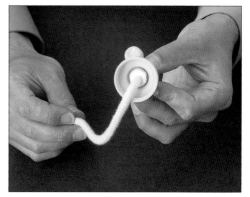

6 In this view you can see that the hole in the collar is the same diameter as the cord, in order to provide the support needed for the trick.

7 Insert the prepared cord into the bottle and screw on the lid.

8 You are now set to make your friends jump out of their skins.

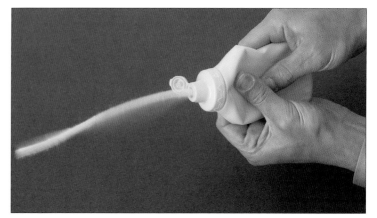

9 When the situation is right, simply squeeze the bottle hard and the string will launch itself out of the bottle, looking exactly like a stream of mustard.

magnetic credit cards

Have you ever wondered what the magnetic strip on the back of a credit card is for? Did you know that if you rub the strip on your sleeve it will become magnetic? It doesn't really, of course, but your spectators will think so when they see what you do with it!

secret view

1 Hold two credit cards and rub the magnetic strips on your sleeves as you explain to the spectators that you are generating static electricity.

2 Bring the two credit cards together, back to back. The card in your right hand should go behind the one in your left hand.

3 Notice how the edge of the credit card is touching the tip of your thumb. Push the cards together and as you do so allow the card to snap off your thumb and on to the other card. It will look and sound as if they are magnetized.

secret view

4 Pull the cards away from each other, reversing the movement and pulling the card against your left thumb.

5 Show the audience that the cards are no longer magnetized. If you wish to involve the audience even more, you can borrow the credit cards from a spectator and hand them back afterwards.

defying gravity

In this easy trick you raise a bottle from the table in a seemingly impossible fashion. No one else will be able to do it, which is likely to *both infuriate and amuse them. Make sure that you use a a coloured bottle with a label on it so they can't see what you are doing.*

secret view

1 Hold your hand in a fist and place it next to a bottle.

2 Touch your fist to the side of the bottle.

3 Lift the bottle off the table, seemingly without gripping it at all.

4 This view makes it clear that as soon as your fist is out of site behind the label your little finger stretches out to provide the necessary grip.

sticky fingers

This trick makes a good follow-up to Defying Gravity. Many objects can be made to cling to your finger using this simple technique. You *will find that some objects will work better than others. Experiment with different items and select the one that works best.*

secret view

1 Point your first finger and touch it to a box of playing cards, a packet of cigarettes, a mobile phone, or any other box-shaped object that you are holding in your left hand.

2 Let go of the box with your left hand. It will cling like a magnet to the first finger of your right hand.

3 This view shows how your little finger extends under the object. It is completely covered by the object and cannot be seen by the spectators.

lighter than light

You strike a match and it floats briefly between your hands. It's best to practise this with an unlit match. You should always take great care when using matches and fire, and children should not attempt this trick unless they are closely supervized by an adult.

1 Take a match from a box and secretly dig the nail of your right middle finger into the base of the matchstick until the wood splits slightly.

2 Steady the match with your thumb and first finger. Now strike it.

3 The match will remain securely wedged on your fingernail.

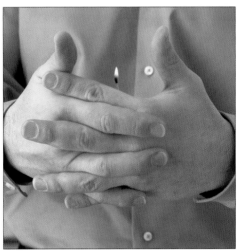

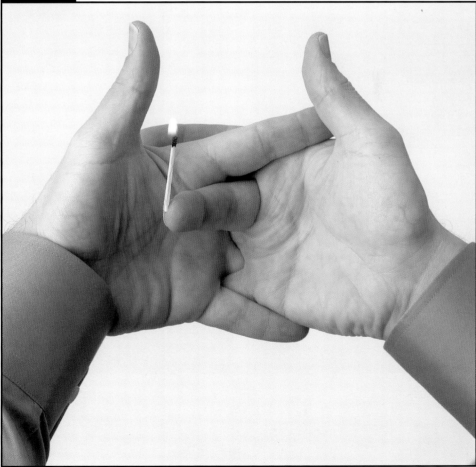

4 Lower your right middle finger and then interlock your fingers as shown. The match will appear to float behind your interlocked fingers.

5 From behind you can see how the finger supporting the match remains hidden from view. This is the secret to the trick. By wiggling your finger you can make the lighted match appear to float from side to side.

finger mouse

A small mouse appears inside your cupped hands and then disappears just as fast. This is a lovely little trick to show young children. If you want to perform this as an impromptu trick, then you should carry the mouse around with you in your pocket.

1 To make the mouse you will need a small piece of brown paper, a black pen, a needle and black thread, a pair of scissors and some adhesive tape.

2 Wrap the paper around your finger to form a cone and hold it together with a small piece of tape.

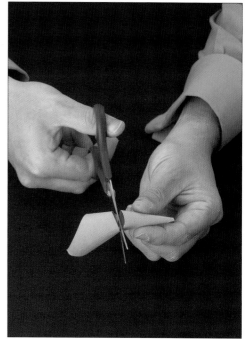

3 Trim off the open end of the cone so it is about 4cm (1½in) long.

4 Draw two eyes and a nose on the mouse with a black pen.

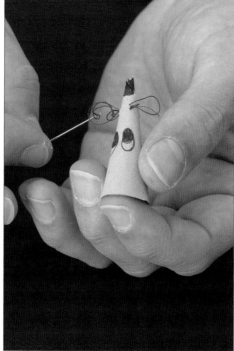

5 Use the needle and thread to make some long loops just above the nose.

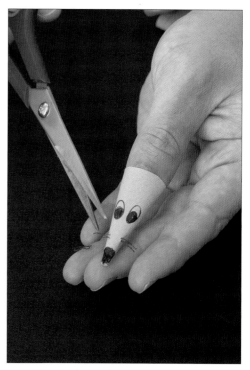

6 Clip the loops into separate strands to create whiskers.

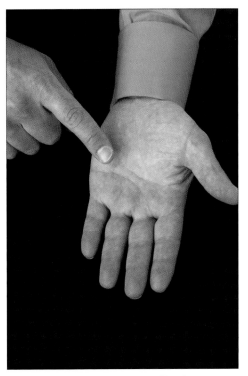

7 To begin the trick, casually show your left hand to be empty. Your right hand points to your empty left palm.

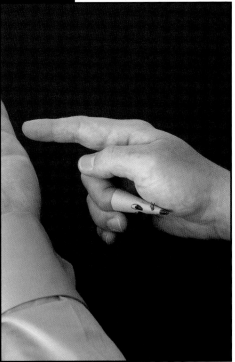

8 The mouse is hidden on the tip of your right middle finger, which is curled inwards. From the front the mouse cannot be seen.

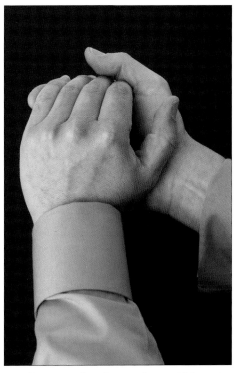

9 Cup your hands together as if there is something inside them.

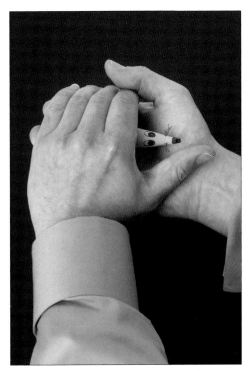

10 Slowly extend your second finger so that the mouse's head pops out from between your hands. Wiggle this finger in and out so that the mouse looks alive.

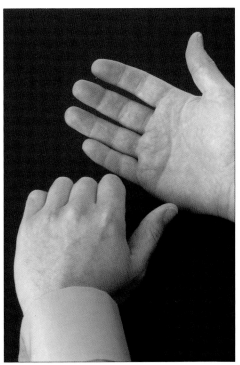

11 To make the mouse disappear, grip it in your closed left fingers and remove your right hand, showing that it is empty.

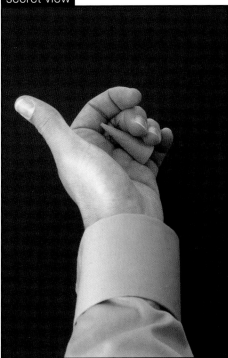

12 The mouse, now held secretly in your left fingertips, can be pocketed without anyone seeing it.

the shirt off your back

You ask for a volunteer and sit them down in front of the spectators. Your helper is wearing a shirt and jacket. You ask them to undo their cuffs and the top few buttons. With a sharp tug you pull off their shirt, *even though they are still wearing their jacket! This trick requires the help of a stooge: in an informal situation like a party this could be a friend who is dressed ready for action.*

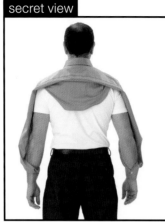

1 An accomplice puts on a shirt in a special way. First, drape it over the shoulders like a cape and button up the top four or five buttons. Then button the sleeves around the wrists.

2 This is how it looks from the back. Try to arrange the shirt neatly so that the fabric is not bunched up in a way that will show through the jacket.

3 Finally put a jacket over the top of the shirt and adjust the clothing so that the shirt looks natural.

4 When you perform the trick, invite the supposedly random volunteer to sit down. Stand behind them and ask them to unbutton the first four buttons of their shirt and their cuffs. The shirt is now loose and all you need to do is pull with one quick jerk to remove the shirt in an apparently impossible manner. If your friend reacts appropriately it can be extremely funny.

tip *To lead into the stunt you can talk about how you recently saw a TV programme on how pickpockets can actually steal the shirt off your back without you noticing! If you have not already done so, check out Tie Through Neck, which could be combined with this trick to make a nice little routine.*

loose thread

When someone tries to pull off the loose thread on your shirt they will get the shock of their life when your shirt starts to unravel! This gag *also works really well on a tie. Never draw attention to the thread; wait for your friend to spot it, then ask them to remove it for you.*

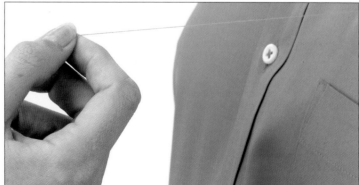

1 Take a 1.2m (4ft) length of thread that is a similar colour to your shirt and thread a short piece through the fabric just above the breast pocket. The remainder of the thread stays inside the shirt. Leave the end hanging and wait!

2 Eventually someone will try to remove the thread for you, and when they pull it the thread will just get longer and longer, as if the stitching is coming undone.

snag!

You supposedly pull a loose thread from a friend's tie and the tie wiggles as though it is being unravelled! This is a really fun gag that is perfect for raising a quick laugh. Don't make a big thing of it however – it is much funnier if you just do it and then move on as if nothing has happened. It is particularly good for a party, or in an office or school where people are wearing ties.

1 Hold the end of the tie in your left hand. Your thumb is on top and your fingers are underneath.

2 The fingers flap up and down very quickly as you mime pulling a thread with your right hand. The end of the tie will flap frantically and should result in a slick gag that will raise an instant smile.

double your money

This clever feat of origami makes a single banknote look like two. It is an ideal trick to perform impromptu if you carry the folded note around with you, and is sure to convince your audience. Just don't let them handle the note or they will discover the truth!

1 To prepare the trick, fold a banknote in half crossways.

2 Open the note and fold it in half again, lengthwise.

3 Pinch the note between each crease with your fingers and thumbs.

4 Flatten the folds on both sides so that the edges all line up.

5 At a glance the folded banknote will look like two notes.

unburstable balloon

We all know what happens when you push a sharp point into a balloon – it goes POP! Well, with this simple stunt you can push sharp *sticks into the balloon without it bursting. This trick can be used as part of a routine with Needles Thru Balloon.*

1 Blow up a balloon and apply two strips of clear adhesive tape in a cross, as shown. Apply another patch on an area directly opposite.

2 Display a sharp wooden skewer in one hand and hold the prepared balloon in the other.

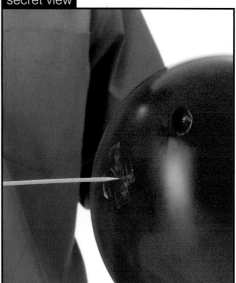

3 Carefully and slowly push the skewer into the balloon, through the centre of the tape cross.

4 Direct the skewer so that it exits from the balloon through the second prepared patch.

5 If you prepare enough tape crosses on the balloon you can use several sticks at once.

obedient handkerchief

A handkerchief moves about at the prankster's command. This can look really funny if your acting skills are good enough. Britain's late *Bob Read performed this better than anyone and always had his audiences in stitches.*

1 Stretch a handkerchief between your hands. You will find that by holding it through your closed left fist it will stand up on end quite easily with 10–12.5cm (4–5in) protruding.

2 With your free hand, pull the handkerchief higher and once again let go. To make it more convincing, look as though you are concentrating on making the handkerchief remain upright.

3 Do this once more until more than half of the handkerchief is upright.

4 With your free hand, motion toward the handkerchief as if you are putting it into a hypnotic trance. Let it fall down, apparently put to sleep as a result of your hypnotic powers.

5 Fold the handkerchief in half and once again hold it with a section raised through your fist.

6 Pretend to pull a hair from your head, perhaps grimacing as you do so.

7 Wrap this invisible hair around the top of the handkerchief and pretend to pull the hair. At the same time, push your thumb up and the handkerchief will bend to the left.

8 Now mime pulling the hair the other way and this time pull down with your thumb and the handkerchief will bend the other way.

milo the mouse

A handkerchief is rolled to resemble a mouse, which then crawls around and eventually jumps out of your hands entirely. This is great if you are entertaining children. The most charming aspect of this party trick is that the mouse is created in front of their very eyes and it is your skill that brings it to life. Children in particular will love this trick – whether they are performing it or being performed to.

1 Start the trick with a handkerchief unfolded in a diamond shape on the table in front of you.

2 Fold the handkerchief diagonally so that the corners are pointing away from you.

3 Fold the right and then the left side of the handkerchief into the centre so that they overlap slightly.

4 Start to roll up the handkerchief from the bottom.

5 Continue rolling until you reach the top of the folded sides.

6 Turn the handkerchief over and fold the right side in to the centre.

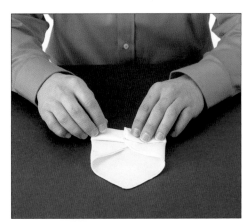

7 Fold over the left side so that the two flaps overlap.

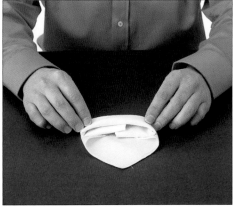

8 Roll upwards from the bottom again until you reach the edge of the folded part of the handkerchief.

9 Tuck the top triangular part of the handkerchief into the gap at the top of the roll.

10 Insert your thumbs into the opening at the bottom and turn the whole thing inside out.

11 Keep turning the handkerchief inside out until two corners appear.

12 Pull out the sides of one of the corners, as shown.

13 Twist the material down towards the rest of the handkerchief.

14 Make a small knot in the two ends of the twist.

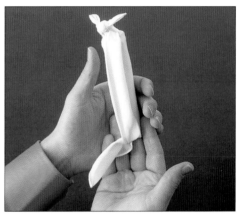

15 Introduce the spectators to Milo the Mouse. To make him move you need to insert your right middle finger into the rolled-up handkerchief under the tail.

16 Stroke the mouse with your left hand as the right fingers flick up and down. The movements, if executed well, make it look as if the mouse is alive.

17 You can even make him crawl up your body and if you give the handkerchief a flick with your right hand you can catch Milo by the tail and pull him back with the left. A good way to finish the routine is to ask someone to stroke Milo. As they approach him give a big flick with your right fingers and send the mouse flying off your hand entirely. If you scream in mock horror as this happens the spectators will jump out of their skin.

blow your nose

You blow your nose into a handkerchief, which flips up into the air. Like many of the pranks in this section, this should be impromptu.

If you call people's attention to such a small joke it will not be as funny as when people see it happen out of the corner of their eye.

secret view

1 Secretly hold a pencil under a handkerchief as you bring the handkerchief to your face.

2 Position the handkerchief as you would if you were going to blow your nose. Under cover of the handkerchief prepare to point the pencil up into the air.

3 Pretend to blow your nose and as you do so flip the pencil up. The handkerchief will rise up in a comical fashion. When you stop blowing your nose let the pencil drop back down and keep it hidden as you put the handkerchief away.

broken arm

As you shake someone's hand your arm makes a bone-crunching noise, which is sure to get a reaction from your unsuspecting victim. A little bit of acting will go a long way to making this prank really

funny. Don't overdo it, just make out that you are in a little pain when the cup is crushed. The louder the noise when the cup is crushed, the better the illusion will be, so experiment with different cups.

secret view

1 Secretly place a disposable plastic cup under your right armpit and shake someone's hand.

2 As you shake their hand crush the cup under your arm so that a horrible crunching sound can be heard.

broken nose

While we are on the subject of broken body parts, here is an audible illusion that will convince people your nose is broken.

secret view

1 Begin the trick by holding both hands palm to palm, covering your nose. Make sure that you are directly face on to the audience.

2 Under cover of your hands, put your thumbnail behind your front tooth. Now bend your hands to the left as if pushing your nose and at the same time click your thumbnail off the tooth. It will sound as though the bone is cracking.

popping your joints

For one last bone breaker, try this out and create the illusion of popping your joints. It is a brilliant illusion and will make people squirm.

secret view

1 Hold a finger as shown here. Gently bend your finger back a couple of times.

2 As you bend your finger a third time simply click the finger and thumb of your right hand underneath. It will sound just as if you are popping your joints loudly.

tip *Believe it or not you can do this to someone else. Just tell them to hold out their hand and click your finger and thumb under their finger. Be sure not to hurt them in any way.*

dead man's finger

This stunt results in a weird and slightly scary sensation. You and a friend can make your fingers instantly feel numb. This is because you are not touching both sides of your finger, but half of your finger and half of the other person's. Furthermore, the back of your finger is not a very sensitive area so you will hardly feel anything on that side. It is hard to appreciate how strange it is until you try it out yourself.

1 Hold hands with someone as shown. Notice how both first fingers are extended.

2 Pinch the first fingers with your finger and thumb and you will get the sensation that your finger is numb.

torn wallpaper

Once you know how to make the simple gimmick you can do this trick anywhere. Experiment with different sized pieces of paper. It is *best to prepare this when nobody is looking and then watch people's faces when they see it – especially the person whose home it is!*

1 Take a piece of white paper and fold it in half. Make the fold with a sharp crease.

2 Tear out a triangular shape from the folded edge. It does not have to be neat. In fact the more jagged the tear, the better the illusion works.

3 Open up the folded paper and curl one half upwards. Wet the back of the straight half with a tiny amount of water and stick it on to a flat surface such as a wallpapered wall or a picture.

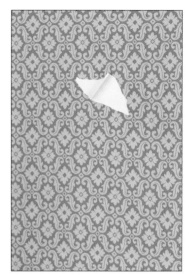

4 At a glance it will look as if the paper has been torn and is peeling away. Try to position the paper so that the folded edge is at an angle and therefore hidden from the direction from which people will see it.

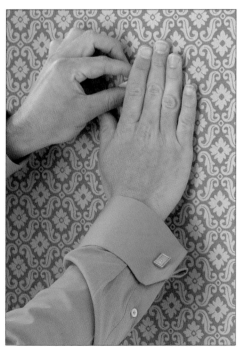

5 When someone finally spots the tear, say that you can fix it. Cover the paper with both hands – the right hand flat and the left preparing to secretly remove the paper from the wall.

secret view

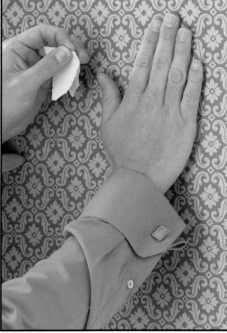

6 The right hand rubs the wallpaper and the left comes away from the wall with the paper hidden inside. (This is an exposed view.)

7 After a few rubs, finish by removing your right hand to show that the wallpaper has been completely restored.

Jacob's ladder

With a little adhesive tape, a few scraps of paper and a pair of scissors you can make an amazing ladder that looks very impressive. Both *this and Jacob's Tree can be made from newspaper rather than coloured paper, although it won't look as nice.*

1 Tape several pieces of paper together to make a long strip. We used five sheets of colourful A4 paper but newspaper would also work well.

2 Roll up the long paper strip into a reasonably tight tube.

3 Use a small amount of adhesive tape to secure the roll.

4 Use a pair of sharp scissors to cut halfway through the width of the tube, about 7.5cm (3in) from either end.

5 Now cut a slit along the length of the tube between the two cuts you have just made.

6 Open out and flatten the tube along the slit. Bend the ends down.

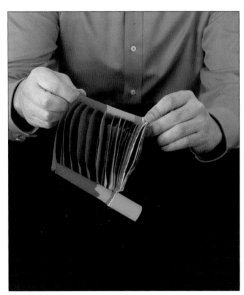

7 Carefully tease out the paper from the tubes on either side and watch the ladder grow before your eyes.

8 The completed ladder is impressive considering it is made so quickly from just a few pieces of paper.

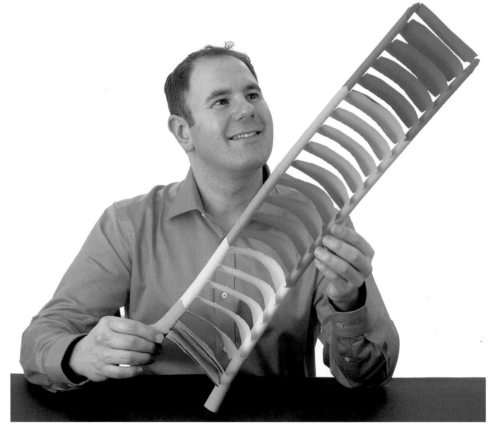

Jacob's tree

This is similar to Jacob's Ladder, except this time you make a tree. Coloured paper is reasonably expensive, so if you want to make a *really huge tree then it may be better to tape sheets of newspaper together so that the trick doesn't cost too much.*

1 Tape five pieces of A4 paper together to make a long strip. Newspaper would also work well.

2 Roll up the coloured paper strip into a reasonably tight tube.

3 Use some adhesive tape to secure the end of the strip.

4 Use a pair of sharp scissors to cut halfway down the length of the tube.

5 Repeat this cut at three other points around the tube.

6 Bend the cut sections down, as shown in the picture.

7 Carefully tease out the paper from the middle of the tube.

8 The completed tree will take shape before your eyes.

bottomless mug

This is a simple gag that makes it look as though there is a hole in the bottom of a mug. It is a quick stunt and fun to do, perhaps as part of *another trick that requires a cup, stick or knife. Despite the simplicity of this party trick, it is very effective and will catch people's attention.*

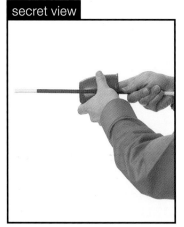

1 Hold a mug in your left hand with the palm up, and the mouth of the mug pointing to the right. Hold a wand, stick or knife in your other hand.

2 Hold the wand, stick or knife with the right first finger extended along its side. Tap inside the bottom of the mug a few times to show that it does not have a hole in it. Each time you tap, remove the wand from the mug and re-insert it.

3 On the third or fourth tap push the wand behind the cup, with your first finger inside the cup. This is the view from the front.

4 This view reveals what is really happening. As soon as the wand passes "through" the bottom of the mug, pull it back out again and hand the mug round for inspection.

relight my fire

In this trick, you show how a blown-out candle can be relit without touching a flame to the wick. This works because the smoke is *combustible. The flame ignites the fumes from the smoke and travels back down the plume to relight the wick.*

1 Position an ordinary candle on a candle holder and light it.

2 Leave it to burn for a couple of seconds, then blow out the flame.

3 Immediately hold a lit match to the smoke from the candle, about 2.5cm (1in) above the wick, and the wick will relight, as if by magic.

floating bread roll

Under the cover of a napkin a bread roll starts to float off the table and away from the dinner guests! This fun and easy-to-perform trick *is a greatly simplified version of a famous magic trick called the "Zombie Floating Ball".*

1 You will need a bread roll, a thick napkin and a fork.

2 Hold the napkin by the top two corners. You can see here that a fork is secretly held behind the napkin between the thumb and index finger of your right hand, parallel to the top of the napkin.

3 The fork is not visible to spectators from the front.

4 Cover the bread roll with the napkin, making sure they do not see the fork.

5 As you do so, stab the prongs of the fork into the roll.

6 Lift the fork upwards and from the front the roll will look as if it is floating underneath the napkin.

7 Make the roll travel left and right, seemingly out of control. This is where your miming and acting abilities come in.

8 Reach up to the roll with your left hand and subtly pull it off the fork.

secret view

9 Bring the roll back to the plate and uncover it, secretly dropping the fork into your lap.

10 With the fork safely hidden you can toss the napkin to the table with a flourish.

bumblebee eggs

You show your friend an envelope, which you say contains a rare breed of bumblebee eggs. When your friend's curiosity gets the better of them and they peek inside the envelope they will jump out of their skin with surprise!

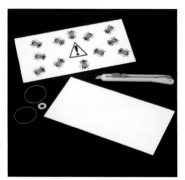

1 You will need two rubber bands, an envelope decorated with bumblebees, a sheet of thick cardboard, a craft knife and a washer.

2 Make a special bumblebee noisemaker by cutting a large hole in the board. Then make two flaps at either end.

3 Attach two rubber bands to a washer.

4 Loop the rubber bands over the flaps in the board.

5 Twist the washer until the bands are wound as tightly as possible and insert the prepared board inside the envelope. The sides of the envelope will stop the washer from unwinding.

6 Show the envelope to your victim and explain that you recently found some bumblebee eggs that are very rare and worth a fortune. Your friend will be eager to see what they look like.

7 When they pull the board out of the envelope, the rubber bands will instantly unwind and the washer will hit the sides of the envelope, making a loud noise that will scare the wits out of your unsuspecting victim.

fake scars

Here are two simple ways to make realistic-looking scars. The techniques are useful for fancy dress parties and to play pranks on *your friends. As you will be using glue, you should make sure that you work over a suitable surface, such as an old cloth or newspaper.*

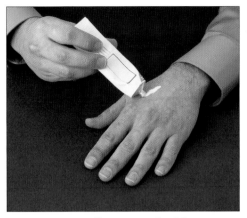

1 Smear a small amount of rubber cement on your skin.

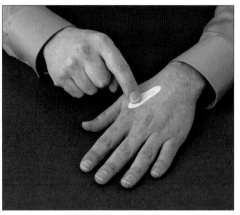

2 Thin it out by rubbing it gently with your fingertip.

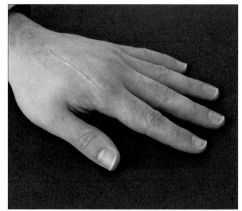

3 When the cement has dried it will become clear. Now pinch the skin in the glued area and a realistic scar will form.

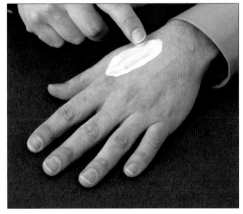

4 Here is another style of scar. Apply a dollop of rubber cement to your skin, as before.

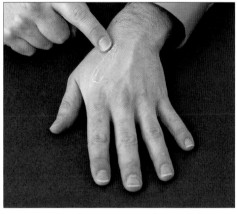

5 Wait for the cement to dry and then roll in the sides.

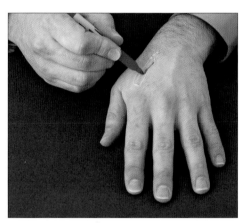

6 For a final touch use a red felt pen to colour the centre.

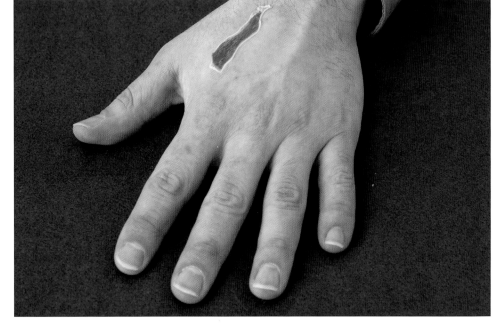

7 The result is a realistic-looking scar that will roll or wash off very easily when you have finished playing pranks on people.

tip *Wait until the cement dries and becomes translucent before creating the folds. You can create the scars on many different parts of your body, but do not put glue near your mouth or eyes.*

invisible coin catch

You hold an empty paper bag open in your right hand and throw an invisible coin into it with your left hand. Although no one can see the *coin, they can hear it when it lands in the bag with an audible thud. This was one of the British comedian Tommy Cooper's favourite stunts.*

secret view

1 Show the audience that a paper bag is empty and hold it with the fingertips of your right hand. Notice how the first and second fingers overlap each other.

2 Throw an imaginary coin up in the air with your left hand and follow with your eyes its imaginary parabola across to the bag.

3 When it is about to reach the bag hold your hand to your ear, non-verbally cuing the spectators to listen.

secret view

4 Flick your second finger off your first finger: the flicking noise against the paper bag will sound exactly like a coin being landing inside.

tip *If you want to show a real coin after it has landed, start the trick with one hidden between your right-hand fingers and the bag. Then, after you have shown the bag empty, let the coin fall silently to the bottom. Continue with the trick and once you have made the snapping noise invite someone to reach inside and remove the coin.*

comedy rising match

You open a box of matches and a match pops up in a comical way. This is sure to raise a smile when you use it. You might be able to *think of a funny picture you could draw on the cover of the box, incorporating the pop-up match.*

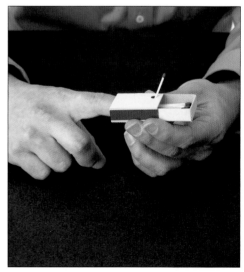

1 Use a hole punch to make a small hole about 6mm (¼in) from the end of the matchbox cover.

2 Close the box and insert a match through the hole so that only the head remains outside the box.

3 Push open the box with your fingertip and the match will pop up through the hole in a comical way.

a good head for money

You stick a coin to a friend's head and they can't shake it off, no matter how hard they try. The reason that they are unable to shake *the coin off is that you have already secretly removed it and hidden it in your hand or in a pocket.*

1 Take a small coin and stick it to your own forehead by pushing quite hard. Now hold your hand out under the coin and knock the back of your head with the other hand.

2 The coin will fall off your forehead after a few bangs.

3 Tell a friend they are not allowed to touch the coin, but all they have to do to dislodge it is bang the back of their head, as you did. Press the coin against their forehead and hold it for about five seconds.

secret view

4 As you remove your hand secretly remove the coin and conceal it in your hand or transfer it to your pocket. You may find this easier if your fingernail is under the coin from the start. As you pushed the coin quite hard your friend will think they can still feel the coin stuck to their head.

5 Of course they can bang their head as much as they like because there is no coin there to fall off.

laughter lines

Trick a friend into covering their face with dirty marks. Be careful not to roll the coin too near the victim's eyes as you don't want lead to get in them. You should also be prepared for quite a dramatic reaction once they realize what you have done!

1 Secretly run the lead of a soft pencil around the edge of a coin. Have an identical clean coin to hand.

2 Give your friend the prepared coin and tell them to copy every move you make with the clean coin. Hold the edge of the coin at the top of your nose and run it down to your chin in a straight line. Next roll it from ear to ear.

3 Continue rolling the coin for as long as you like. By the time your friend has finished their face will look a complete mess!

matchbox challenge

It sounds easy to drop a matchbox from a short height and have it land on its end, but no one will be able to do it unless they know the secret. It may take a few attempts to perfect the technique, but once you've got the hang of it you should succeed every time.

secret view

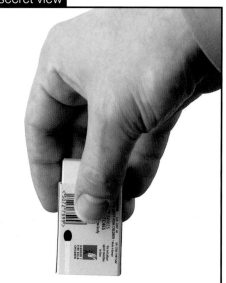

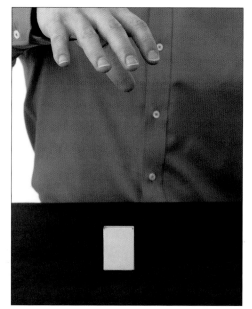

1 Hold a matchbox between the tips of your right fingers approximately 15cm (6in) above the table.

2 You have secretly pushed about 1cm (⅜in) of the drawer out. It is hidden by the backs of your fingers.

3 Let the matchbox drop: it will land on end. When anyone else tries it they will fail, as the matchbox will bounce and fall over.

tie through neck

After calling attention to your tie you give it a quick tug and it passes through your neck, leaving your head still attached to your shoulders.

You could set this trick up with a friend and then follow it with The Shirt Off Your Back, making a nice impromptu-looking routine.

1 Without putting it round your neck, knot the tie neatly leaving a large loop at the back, which you flatten to form two flaps.

2 Feed both flaps around the collar, then fold the collar down to hold the flaps in position.

3 With the collar neatly in position the tie will look normal. When you are ready to have some fun, point out your tie and give it a sharp tug downwards.

4 It will look just as though the tie has passed right through your neck.

beer money

A banknote lies trapped beneath an upturned bottle. The challenge is to remove the banknote without the bottle falling over. The bottle

must not be touched at any time. This trick must be performed on a smooth surface or it will not work.

   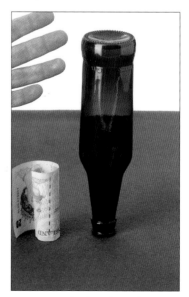

1 Set an empty glass bottle upside down on top of a banknote.

2 Carefully roll up the banknote from one end.

3 As you continue to roll the banknote, the bottle will gradually slide off the other end of the note.

4 Once the bottle is clear of the banknote you can pick it up and pocket it.

smiling Queen

This quirky trick with a British banknote uses origami to make the picture of the Queen smile or frown. You may well be able to find a *banknote of a different currency for which this technique works too – try it out on various currencies to see.*

1 Place a banknote in front of you with the Queen's head uppermost.

2 Make a sharp vertical fold precisely through the Queen's right eye.

3 Now make another sharp fold through the Queen's left eye.

4 Make a final fold between the previous two in the opposite direction, so that the banknote looks like this.

5 If you open the banknote and look down from the top, the Queen looks as if she is frowning slightly.

6 As you tilt the note away from you and look up at it the Queen slowly begins to smile.

origami rose

A paper napkin is twisted and folded to resemble a beautiful and realistic rose. While this is not a magic trick, it is a great origami model to remember. People always enjoy watching the rose being made, and they can also keep it as a memento of the evening.

1 This works best using a single layer of thin paper. So if you have a multi-ply napkin, strip one layer from it.

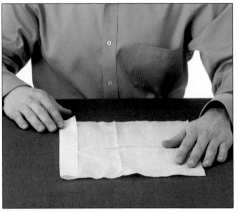

2 Lay the napkin in front of you and fold over a strip 3cm (1³⁄₁₆in) wide down one side.

3 Hold the top of the fold between the first and second fingers of your right hand and roll the paper over your fingers along the fold until you reach the end.

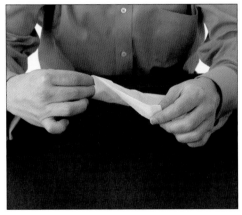

4 Ensure that this is done neatly, as it will form the head of the rose.

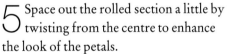

5 Space out the rolled section a little by twisting from the centre to enhance the look of the petals.

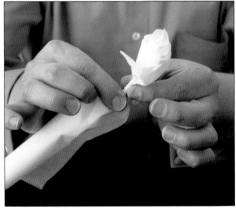

6 Pinch and twist the tissue just below the folded section to form the top of the stem.

7 Once you have twisted about 2.5cm (1in) of the stem, take hold of a corner of the napkin from the bottom.

8 Pull this corner about halfway up the stem to form a single leaf and tightly twist the rest of the napkin below it to complete the stem.

9 Adjust the folds as necessary to produce a perfect paper rose.

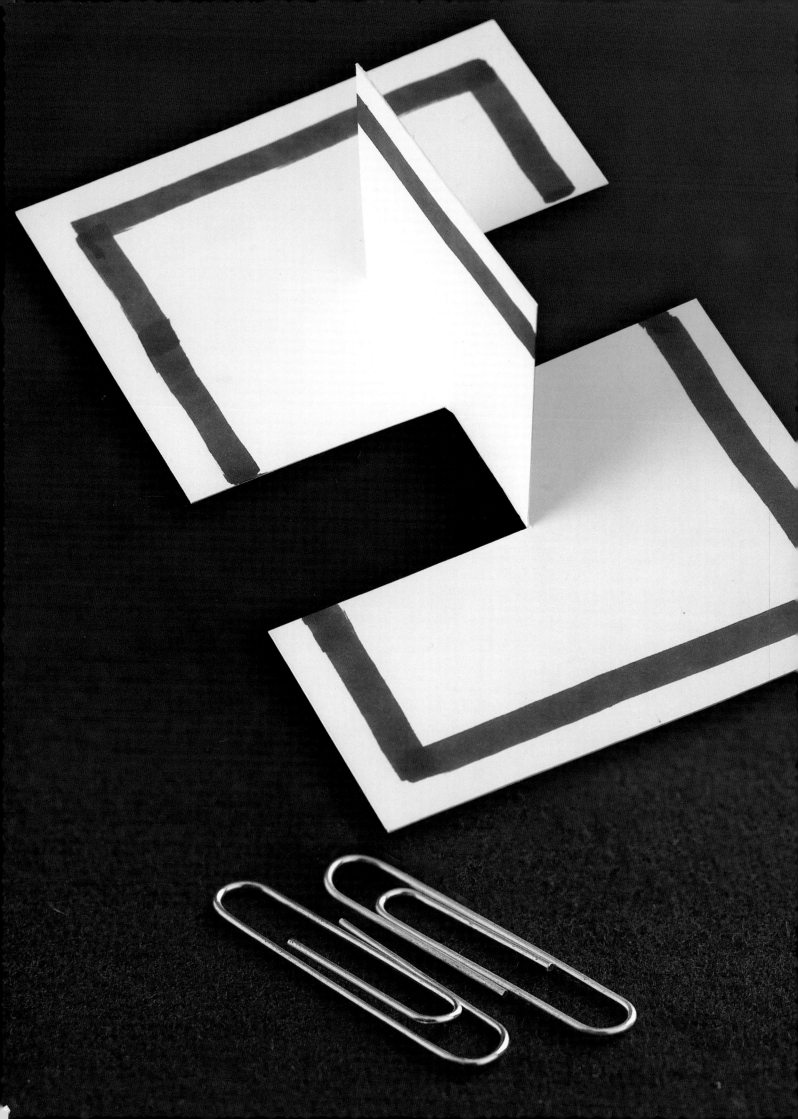

optical illusions

This chapter contains a variety of optical illusions, including two-dimensional images that will confuse your brain, and those that require your input to make the illusions happen. Those that can be performed make ideal party tricks, or can be incorporated into a stand-up show to add an extra dimension. One thing is certain, as you proceed through this chapter you'll find it hard to believe your eyes!

introduction

How we see things, and how we interpret the images we see, is ultimately determined by two organs– our eyes and our brain. It has been said many times that "seeing is believing", but magic tricks and optical illusions achieve their effects by defying this otherwise rational comment.

The brain is the most complex organ in the body. Everything the body does is linked to messages sent to and from the brain through approximately 100 billion nerve cells. There are two sides to the human brain, the left hemisphere and the right hemisphere. While the left side of the brain deals with all things logical, such as mathematics, speech, writing and reading, the right side of the brain tends to dominate when we are dealing with more creative processes, such as storytelling, artistic pursuits, acting, imagination or dreaming.

Occasionally, we see an image with our eyes that our brain cannot make sense of. This may be due to the fact that while the right side of the brain is creating an image, the left side of the brain is simultaneously trying to find some logic in what we are looking at to explain an apparent anomaly. This clash of thoughts seems to cause the confusion that ensues.

Above: Water sometimes has a strange effect on our perceptions of depth and distance. Here, the boat appears to be floating in mid air rather than on the surface of the crystal clear water.

Below: Mirages that occur in deserts are amazing natural optical illusions that have been known to drive people lost in the desert to madness. The mirage appears as liquid, but those desperate for a drink can never reach the water.

We can often see natural optical illusions all around us. For example, have you ever seen a mirage in a desert? If not, you may have seen a similar phenomenon on a road on a hot summer's day.

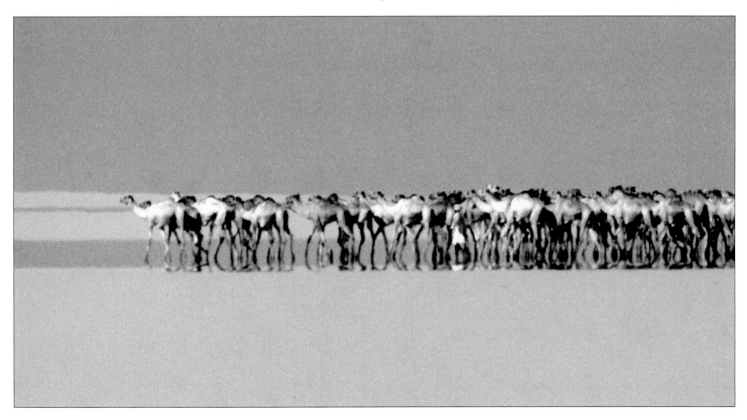

When the sun is beating down on the sand or road it heats it to an extreme level; the heat then rises from the surface and creates a layer of hot air that reflects the light in a different way to the slightly cooler air above it. These reflections are visible to the human eye, as the layer of air acts like a mirror reflecting the sky above, creating the illusion of a pool of water shimmering in the sun.

Another common optical illusion can be seen if you look at the wheel of a car when it is moving fast. The hubcap seems to be turning in the opposite direction to the wheel. And have you ever been sitting on a stationary train when the train next to you slowly starts to move? You sometimes get the weird sensation that *you* are moving backwards and that the other train is standing still.

Of all the artists who have specialized in creating optical illusions in art, the Dutch graphic artist M. C. Escher (1898–1972) was perhaps one of the most famous, using tricks of perspective to draw "impossible objects", which could not exist in three dimensions, although at first sight they seem to make sense.

In more recent times, the British pavement artist Julian Beever, who is based in Belgium, has been gaining worldwide fame as photographs of his unbelievable works of art are sent to millions via email. His chalk drawings often work from just one particular angle, but from that optimum viewing point he creates unique, original and believable three-dimensional images. Viewed from other angles, it can be seen that the drawings are in fact distorted.

One of the most famous optical illusions in art is Salvador Dali's *Reflections of Elephants*. In this wonderful painting the reflections of three swans swimming on a lake form the images of three elephants – the effect of which is quite remarkable.

Magicians often take advantage of optical illusions. For instance, the way props are painted can suggest that a box is smaller than it really is, and this means that there can be enough room to hide something or someone inside.

In this chapter you will discover some fascinating optical illusions that you can enjoy immediately, while others require some physical input from you in order to make the illusions happen. You may well find that you can incorporate some of these simple but effective illusions with your magic tricks to enhance your presentation, but they are also great fun to try out on your friends. Enjoy the sensation of these illusions and look around you next time you are out and about to see if you can spot other natural optical illusions.

Right: Believe it or not both people are real and there are no camera tricks. This clever illusion by Julian Beever uses perspective to make the man look small when he is simply far away from the camera: the bottle is actually sketched on the ground and is around 9m (30ft) long.

common optical illusions

There are many different types of optical illusion, some of which occur naturally, and others that have been created. Certain optical illusions trick the brain into believing that objects are smaller or larger than another object of the same size. Others are images that can be viewed in more than one way. They all distort our ability to apply rational thinking to a given problem.

which is longer?

Although the top line appears to be shorter than the bottom line, they are in fact the same length. This is called the Müller-Lyer illusion, and was first made famous in 1889.

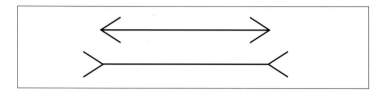

how many shelves?

Can you see three shelves or four shelves? How many you see depends whether you look from the left or the right.

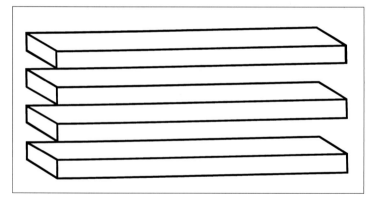

shrinking haze

If you stare at the spot in the middle of the grey haze, the haze will appear to shrink.

small, medium, large

Take a look at these three images. Which do you think is the tallest – 1, 2 or 3? Actually they are all identical. The converging lines distort the images and as the lines get closer together the images seem to grow.

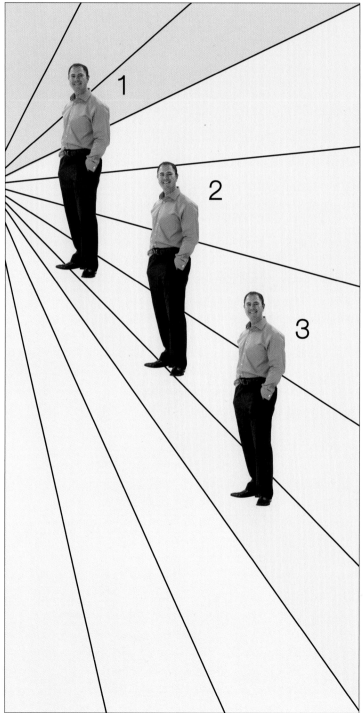

connecting line

In this rather odd optical illusion it is difficult to work out which of the bottom two lines connects with the top line. Use a ruler or straight edge to check which line does join the top one.

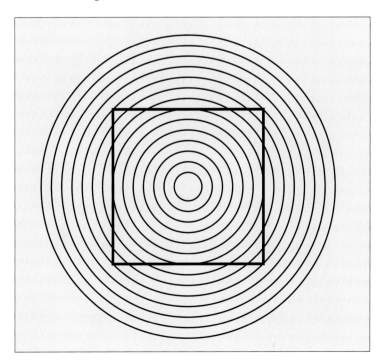

full to the brim

Is the hat below taller than it is wide? Or wider than it is tall? Both the width and the height are actually identical, although you probably won't believe it until you check with a ruler!

all square

Have a look at the square below. Are the sides parallel? Are they perfectly straight or do the sides bow in? Believe it or not all of the sides are straight. The concentric circles appear to "pull" the lines inwards creating the illusion that the sides are bowed.

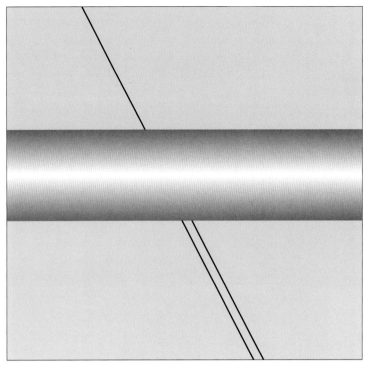

odd ball

This optical illusion is similar to All Square. The smaller circle looks as though it is not perfectly circular, although in reality it is. The rays emanating from the centre distort the outline and make us perceive the circle as irregular.

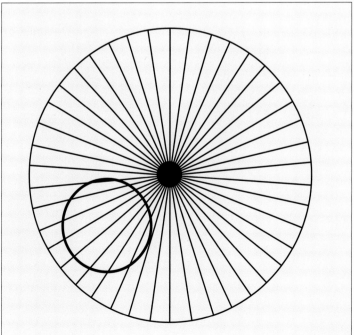

straight or crooked?

Take a look at the lines below. Even though they look like they converge in both directions, they are in fact absolutely parallel! Check with a ruler, if you like.

scintillating illusion

Look at this image for a couple of seconds. Do you see flickering black dots at the intersections of the squares? This effect, called scintillation, was first observed and reported in the early 19th century.

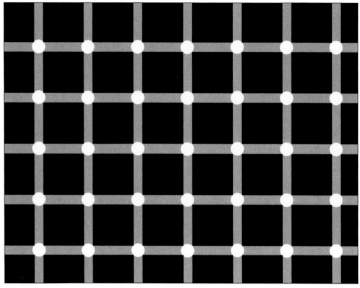

parallel lines

Are the horizontal lines parallel or do they slope? They are actually absolutely parallel, but the offset squares create the optical illusion that the lines converge and in some places bulge. This effect is sometimes seen on tiled walls or floors.

Inuit or Warrior?

Have a look at this picture. What do you see? Hint: The Native American warrior is facing the left, the Inuit is facing the right.

young or old woman?

What do you see when you look at this famous optical illusion? Hint: The old woman's nose is the young woman's cheek.

rabbit or duck?

Which do you see, a rabbit or a duck? This famous illusion is thought to have been drawn by psychologist Joseph Jastrow in 1899.

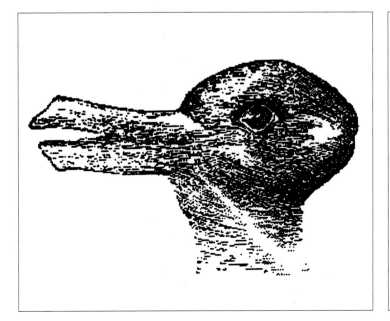

towards or away?

Is this open book facing towards you or away from you? There is no correct answer to this simple optical illusion.

shrinking pen

This fascinating optical illusion makes a pen or pencil shrink in size before your eyes. Watch yourself in the mirror and you will see how good it looks. The illusion is best when it is viewed from the front.

This is a quick and easy illusion that can easily be incorporated into a magic show, or simply demonstrated at a party. It works best if the pen is a different colour to the top that you are wearing.

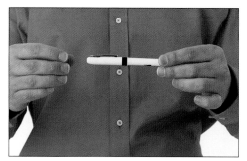
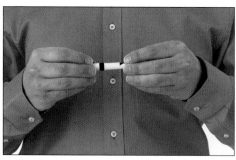
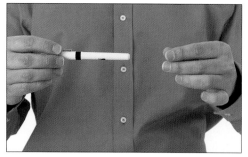

1 Hold a pen in your left fingertips so that your left hand covers just under one-third of the pen when viewed from the front.

2 Now transfer the pen to the fingertips of the right hand.

3 The right hand's grip is identical to the left hand's grip. If these movements are repeated at a speed of about four transfers per second the pen seems to shrink when viewed from the front.

floating sausage

This popular illusion is an example of a stereogram. This effect occurs when two images, one from each of your eyes, are incorrectly combined in your brain, causing them to overlap and – in this case – create a third finger floating between the two real fingers.

Hold the tips of your first fingers about 1cm (½in) apart and about 20cm (8in) from your eyes. Now stare at your fingers and bring them slowly towards the tip of your nose. You will see a sausage-like shape floating in the air between your fingers. There is of course nothing there. What you are seeing are the fingertips of each hand in reverse (as you are crossing your eyes). The result is a sausage shape where the two images overlap.

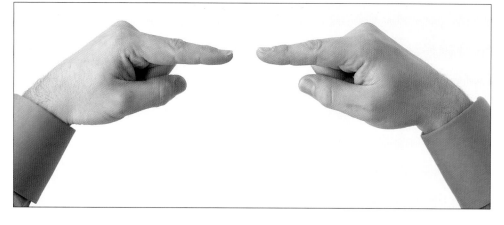

hole in hand

With a piece of paper or card you can create an instant x-ray machine that enables you to see straight through your hand as if there were a hole in the middle of it.

Take a piece of paper or card (stock) and roll it into a tube. Hold the tube to your right eye with your right hand and keep both eyes open. Now hold up your left hand beside the tube with the palm towards you, and you'll see a hole appear in it!
 This is another example of a stereorgam illusion, which occurs when your brain fuses two images, one from each eye, to create a single, combined image.

ship in a bottle

On one side of a piece of card draw a ship, on the other side draw a bottle. Simply by rotating the card you can make it look as though the ship is inside the bottle. The images move so fast that they are *retained for a fraction of a second in the mind's eye, thus merging together to become a single picture. You could try this illusion using other pictures, such as a bird in a cage, or maybe a goldfish in a bowl.*

1 To create this optical illusion you will need a piece of card (stock) measuring 7.5 x 5cm (3 x 2in), a pen, a hole punch and two rubber bands.

2 Punch a hole centrally at each end of the card.

3 Push a rubber band through each hole, and loop one end through the other to attach them, as shown.

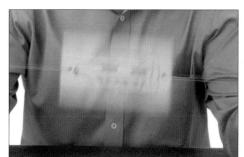

4 On one side of the card draw a big, empty bottle.

5 On the other side of the card draw a ship. The images must be centred and the ship must be small enough to fit inside the bottle. If you hold the card up to the light you will be able to check that the positions are correct.

6 Hold a rubber band in each hand and quickly twist the card back and forth. The spectator will see the ship appear inside the bottle.

Emily's Illusion

I discovered this illusion while playing with one of my daughter's toys. It is a good example of how our eyes are slower to see than we *think. Just like Ship in a Bottle, here the human eye sees two images and blurs them into one.*

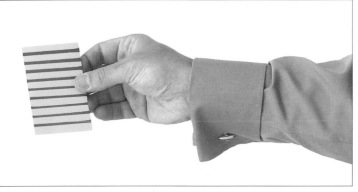

1 Draw thick parallel lines across the width of a piece of card (stock). Hold it at your fingertips.

2 Throw the card up in the air, spinning it as fast as you can. Notice how the lines seem to be going in two directions. It seems that the card has a checked rather than a lined pattern on it.

stretching arm

As you pull your arm it seems to stretch in the most peculiar way. Of course your arm is not actually stretching, but the effect is *surprisingly effective. If you reverse the moves you can also appear to make your arm shrink back to its normal length.*

1 You need to be wearing a long-sleeved shirt for this illusion. Stand up, with your left side to the spectators, then raise your left arm in front of you. Ensure your elbow is slightly bent and that your sleeve is pulled right down to your wrist.

2 Pull your left wrist with your right hand and stretch your arm just a little. Your sleeve will stay where it is but your arm will move forward.

3 Repeat this movement in short bursts, moving your left shoulder forward slightly as you do so.

pinkie down

The little finger of your left hand shrinks until it is tiny. The more slowly you perform this illusion the more amazing it is. American *magician Meir Yedid performs a whole act in which each of his fingers appears to shrink and then disappear, one by one.*

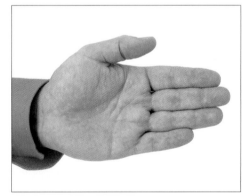

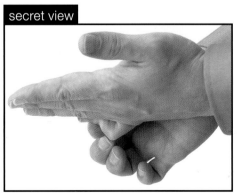

1 Hold your left hand out flat, palm facing the spectators.

secret view

2 Grip your little finger with your right thumb covering all but the last 6mm (¼in) at its tip. Wrap the fingers of your right hand around the back of your left hand.

3 Slide your right hand back and as you do, so bend the little finger at the joint, but ensure that its pad stays in line with the rest of your left hand. Keep sliding the thumb back until you can go no further. It will look as if your little finger is shrinking. Reverse the action to stretch it back to normal size.

4 This is an exposed view of how your hand looks from beneath.

thumb stretch

You hold the tip of your thumb in your teeth and stretch it until it is more than twice as long as it was before! All the moves happen very *fast and the stretched thumb is seen for only about half a second. Of course, the illusion must only be viewed from the front.*

1 Hold your left thumb to your mouth and lightly bite the very tip of it.

2 Bring your right hand up and insert the tip of the right thumb in your mouth, exchanging thumb tips. Reposition your left thumb inside your right fist.

3 Now stretch out your right thumb (with a groan of pain) and simultaneously pull your left thumb out of your right fist, creating the illusion that it has stretched.

secret view

4 From the side you can see what is really happening. Now reverse the moves and finish in the same position you started in.

thumb off

You apparently unscrew the top of your thumb and then screw it back on. This is one of the oldest and most popular tricks in existence *and you may have seen it done before. However, few people do it properly. When done well it is an amazing optical illusion.*

1 Form a circle with the thumb and index finger of your right hand and insert your left thumb into the hole.

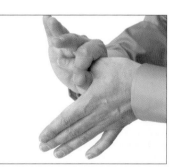

2 Twist your left hand back and forth, explaining to the audience that you are unscrewing your thumb.

secret view

3 With a quick shake of your hands adjust them by bending in your left and right thumbs. Then use your right forefinger to cover the area where the thumbs meet. This is an exposed view.

4 From the front the illusion is perfect. Wiggle the tip of your right thumb, which people will assume is still your left thumb.

5 Now slide your right hand along the side of your left forefinger. Slide it back again.

6 Finish with a quick shake of the hands to readjust them to the position in step 2, as you supposedly screw your thumb back on.

impossible!

A piece of card is placed on the table. It has three cuts in it, yet the spectator cannot work out how the shape is formed from one piece of card alone. This is a very clever trick and is guaranteed to baffle most people the first time they try to work out how it is done.

1 Take a plain piece of card (stock) approximately 12.5 x 7.5cm (5 x 3in) and fold it in half lengthwise. With a pair of scissors, cut a slit from the middle of one edge to the central fold, then turn the card round and cut two more slits on either side of the first slit from the opposite edge.

2 Holding the right half of the card steady, twist the left half through 180 degrees.

3 Fold down the centre section and you will have a most interesting optical puzzle: a shape that seems impossible to form from a single piece of card.

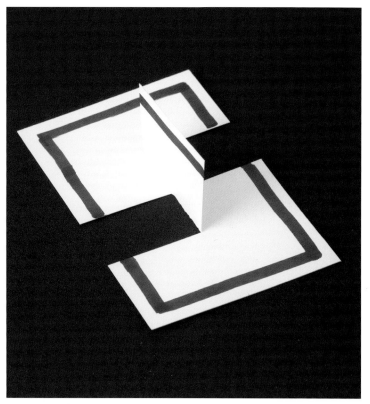

4 To add a really convincing touch, draw a border around the edge with a thick felt-tipped pen and then fold over the centre flap and draw the border across the gap too.

5 This is how it should look when it is finished, and it is ready to try out on people.

boomerang cards

Two boomerang-shaped cards are displayed side by side and it is clear that one is longer than the other. Yet, as you move them around, the cards seem to change size so that the smaller one becomes bigger and vice versa. Try it and discover for yourself how convincing it is.

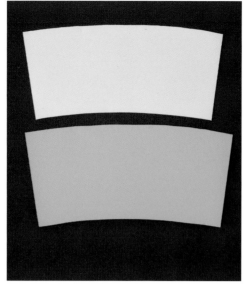

1 Cut out two cards of identical size and shape, as shown here. Use two different colours if you wish.

2 Place one card above the other, curving down. The card at the bottom will look bigger.

3 Pick up the top card and move it to the bottom. Amazingly, it now looks as if it is the bigger one.

4 Try drawing a stick man on each card. The focus is then on the drawings rather than the cards themselves.

5 Switch the positions of the cards slowly and the illusion seems to happen right before your eyes!

stamp it out!

In this clever optical illusion the principle known as refraction, or the bending of light, is responsible for making a stamp disappear from *underneath a glass. Try it out with the props in front of you and you will appreciate just how clever and amazing this illusion is.*

1 You will need a small jug (pitcher) of water, a glass (the taller the better) and a postage stamp. Place the stamp under the glass.

2 Slowly pour water into the glass until it is almost full. Watch the stamp and you will see it disappear.

3 If you look straight down into the glass from above you can still see the stamp, so if you want to stop people from doing this place a plate on top of the glass after you have poured the water. It is now invisible from all angles.

tip *If you want to make this into a magic trick, you could prepare the face of the stamp with double-sided tape so it adheres to the glass. In this way you can lift the glass at the end and the stamp really will be gone from the table!*

east meets west

The direction of an arrow, drawn on a piece of paper can be changed without touching it, but how? Water bends light and refracts it in a *weird and wonderful way. This experiment shows just how strange nature can sometimes be.*

1 Fold a piece of card (stock) in half and draw a large arrow on one side. Stand the card up on the table.

2 Place a glass in front of the card and view the arrow through the glass.

3 To change the arrow's direction simply pour some water into the glass.

two in one

Two glasses are shown to contain liquid. Tell the spectators that the question is whether the contents of both glasses will fit into just one glass? Although it looks impossible you prove that you can indeed fit the contents of both glasses into one.

1 To set up this stunt you need two identical conical glasses. Fill one to the brim and then pour half its contents into the other glass. The illusion is perfect. It seems very unlikely that all that liquid will fit into just one glass but of course you know it can.

2 Slowly pour all of the liquid from the full conical glass to the empty conical glass.

3 Amazingly all of the liquid fits into one glass. The optical illusion is created by the shape of the glass. The wider part at the top can hold far more liquid than the same depth lower down the glass. It is very deceptive.

height of failure

You ask someone to guess which is longer, the circumference of the mouth of a glass or the height of the glass. It is easier to understand how this optical illusion works if you imagine a football field: it's *obvious that running all the way around the edge back to where you started is far longer than running straight down the field once. The same principle is at work here.*

1 This illusion works best if you use a reasonably short glass with a wide mouth. Pose the question: "Which do you think is longer, the height of the glass or the circumference?" Most people will initially guess the height.

2 You can now raise the glass on objects such as boxes, books, playing cards and wallets, until it is really high.

3 Add these things slowly, each time posing the question: "Now which do you think is longer?"

4 Each time you add something the spectators will probably still think that the height is longer, although the circumference is really still quite a bit longer.

5 You can prove this by winding string around the circumference and holding your finger to mark the length.

6 Then hold the string up against the glass to compare lengths.

clip the Queen

As easy as it seems, spectators will not be able to put a paperclip on the Queen card when you present it to them turned face down. Even when you know how the trick works it is very difficult to put the

paperclip on the correct card. This is an easy trick to make up and is fun to keep in your bag ready for those occasions when someone asks you to do an impromptu trick.

1 Glue five old playing cards together in a fan. They should all be spot cards except for the middle card, which should be a Queen.

2 Hold the fan of cards face up and ask someone to remember where the Queen is. Give them a paperclip.

3 Turn the fan face down and ask them to put the paperclip on the card they think is the Queen. It is most likely that they will put the paperclip on the centre card.

4 When you turn the fan over again you will see the paperclip is quite a distance away from the Queen.

5 In order to find the Queen the paperclip needs to be in a position you just wouldn't expect, and people certainly won't think of it the first time they see this.

shrinking wand

Make a magic wand shrink until it disappears completely. The wand is then found inside a tiny matchbox. This optical illusion can easily be used as a trick as part of a larger show. The shrinking principle is one that is used in many tricks, including big stage illusions.

1 Prepare a matchbox drawer by cutting a rectangle out of the bottom. Put this drawer back in the box and keep it in your left pocket.

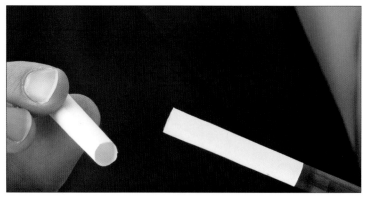

2 Prepare your magic wand by slipping a white tube of paper over one end. The tube should be the same length as the white tip of the wand and loose enough to slide along easily.

3 Display the wand, holding each end at the fingertips with the sliding tube covering the end in your right hand.

4 Slowly move your hands towards each other. The right fingers slide the paper tube down the wand.

secret view

5 The end of the wand starts to go up your sleeve, as shown here. The audience will not be able to see this.

6 From the front the wand looks as if it is shrinking. Make suitable facial expressions so that it is more convincing.

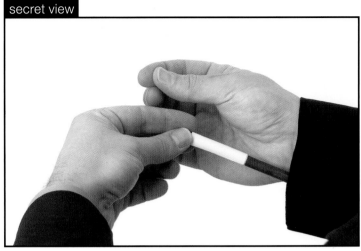

7 When the wand gets really short, start shaking your hand up and down while secretly pushing the entire wand up your sleeve. The smaller motion of pushing the wand up your sleeve will be covered by the larger up-and-down motion of the hands.

8 Hold your empty hands up to show the audience that the wand has disappeared from sight.

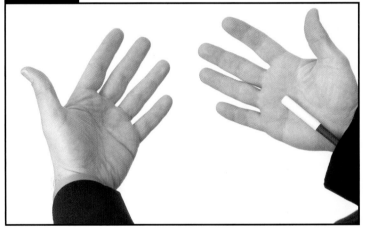

9 The wand is hidden up your sleeve and the end is hidden behind your hand.

10 To make the wand reappear, show the prepared matchbox, holding it in your left fingertips.

11 Transfer the box to your right hand and open it, making sure that the hole in the bottom remains hidden from your audience.

12 Reach into the matchbox, grasp the end of the wand through the hole and slowly pull it out.

13 The illusion is perfect. It looks as if a long wand is magically coming out of a tiny box!

stunts and puzzles

This chapter will test your ability to think laterally and logically. All of the puzzles require a degree of patience and thought, and once you have learnt the answers you can try setting the problems for other people. Some of the amazing stunts will make you look much cleverer than you actually are, while others will give you a huge advantage when issuing a simple challenge or bet.

introduction

A *stunt* is a feat displaying unusual strength, skill or daring. These can range in scale from the very small to the very large. One of the most famous magicians known for his large-scale stunts was none other than the great showman Harry Houdini (1874–1926). In order to promote his forthcoming shows at theatres across the world he would often challenge the local police to lock him up in their apparently "escape-proof" handcuffs. He would then generate immense publicity by promptly escaping from them.

There is a wonderful story that dates from 1904, when Houdini visited London. He was challenged to escape from a pair of cuffs that had been specially commissioned by *The Daily Illustrated Mirror* and were said to have taken five years to design and make. The event took place at the London Hippodrome and garnered huge editorial space from the *Mirror* (presumably selling lots of papers for them) and at the same time ensuring that Houdini was very much in the media spotlight.

Houdini managed to escape from the "Mirror Cuffs" in just over an hour, and the watching crowd went crazy. There are those who believe that the whole stunt was a set-up designed to be mutually beneficial to both the newspaper and Harry Houdini. Could the cuffs, apparently made to withstand escape, have been secretly fixed so that Houdini could open them without a key? Either way, the stunt succeeded in its purpose and it is easy to imagine the kind of sensation it would have caused at the time.

In recent years, the American showman David Blaine has resurrected the genre of publicity stunts. In one of his latest enterprises, in 2003, he starved himself for 44 days, sealed inside a 2 x 2 x 1m (7 x 7 x 3ft) transparent box suspended over London's Tower Bridge, and in New York, in 2006, he unsuccessfully attempted to spend a week submerged in a water-filled sphere. These dangerous stunts have earned him millions of dollars and worldwide fame. The stunts you will learn in this chapter are unlikely to earn you millions or make you famous and are a little more modest than Houdini's or Blaine's. However, they are still a lot of fun to perform and for your friends to witness.

When you think of puzzles, a number of images may spring to mind. There are jigsaw puzzles, puzzles that require lateral thinking, even puzzles made of wire of the kind found in Christmas crackers. You could even say that magic tricks are puzzles, since every magic trick, like a puzzle, has a solution. The major difference between the two is that the solution to a magic trick should always remain hidden, and while the spectator may wonder about how the trick works, it should not be necessary to know this in order to appreciate the value of the trick.

A magic trick often incorporates humour and a degree of entertainment; a puzzle is designed to test the brain, and thoughtful analysis is usually required in order to solve it successfully. That is not to say that puzzles cannot be fun or entertaining. Indeed many of the puzzles in this chapter will be the source of much enjoyment as you try to find solutions and present the puzzles to your friends.

There are some puzzles that require no interaction at all. They are simply visual treats for us to enjoy. A classic example is a ship in a bottle. It seems

Left: Jeff Scanlan's impossible bottles include this amazing creation, in which a large glass container with a narrow spout is packed with 13 tennis balls, each with a circumference bigger than that of the spout.

impossible that such an object could ever have been assembled, but there it is before us and we are intrigued by the conundrum of how it could have been made.

Very often there is more than one way to arrive at the solution to such a puzzle. In the case of the ship in the bottle, the bottom of the bottle might be removed; the ship inserted into the resulting hole and the base of the bottle resealed by a glassblowing expert. Another solution would be to construct the ship from pieces small enough to fit through the neck of the bottle, joining the individual pieces once they are inside. Of course this would require a steady hand and a lot of patience. Yet another solution is to construct a ship that has hinged masts, so that the whole thing can fit through the neck of the bottle with the masts and sails down. Once the ship is inside the bottle the sails can be carefully pulled upright and glued into position.

How would you go about getting a fully grown apple inside a bottle? This feat is actually possible, although it is a little impractical, and you need access to an apple tree in order to do it. All you do is tie the neck of a bottle to the twig of an apple tree at the beginning of the growing season and wait until the apple grows inside the bottle before carefully removing it from its stem. This leaves you with a real, fully grown apple inside a real glass bottle. Of course, before long the apple will begin to rot, so if you go to the trouble of doing this you should show as many people as possible as quickly as you can.

The world's most famous creator of impossible bottles was Harry Eng (1932–96). He managed to insert all kinds of objects into bottles, including scissors, decks of cards, ping-pong balls, golf balls, packs of cigarettes, padlocks, tennis balls, baseballs, books, dice and even a pair of shoes! Harry's work inspired Jeff Scanlan, an American who assembles a wide range of impressive impossible bottles. In some cases he has developed new techniques to create original masterpieces, some of which take weeks to make and seem totally impossible.

On the pages that follow you will find over fifty stunts and puzzles that will test your problem-solving abilities and show off various skills. Some are easier than others and some are really effective. Be warned: many of the most impressive stunts require lots of practice, just like magic tricks.

follow the leader

No matter how closely people follow your movements they are unlikely to be able to replicate what you do here. While you will succeed every time, most of your audience start off with their fingers in the wrong position and will therefore fail to replicate your actions.

1 Tell everyone to copy every move you make. Cross your arms in front of you, hold your hands palm to palm and interlock your fingers. The key to this trick is to make sure that the right arm goes over the left and the right little finger is on top.

2 Now bring your hands in to your chest and up towards your face. Stick out your first fingers.

3 Explain to the audience that you must use the back of the first finger of each hand to touch either side of your nose. This is quite awkward, but entirely possible.

4 Finally, without taking your fingers off your nose, you untwist your fingers and open your arms to reach the position shown.

still following the leader

Again, tell everyone to copy every move you make. Hold your hands out in front of you, palm to palm, and interlock your fingers. As the others copy you, unlock your fingers and comment that the right arm should be over the left (use your hands to gesture as you speak, to justify taking your hands apart). This excuse enables you to reposition your arms as follows.

1 When you interlock your fingers again, twist your left hand anti-clockwise instead of clockwise, so that when your hands come together, although it looks as if your arms are crossed as they were before, they aren't really.

2 Tell the spectators to follow your movements. Slowly give your hands a quarter turn clockwise, bringing you to the position shown. Everyone else will be in a muddle and won't be able to replicate your simple move.

tip *If you find it difficult to get into the position in step 1, simply lock your hands together as in step 2 and twist your hands anti-clockwise until you can't turn them any more. This is the position you need to get into.*

hypnotic, magnetic fingers

You apparently hypnotize your subjects as you demonstrate how the power of the mind can cause the body to do things against its will, making the volunteer's fingers close together involuntarily.

Although this stunt is not really hypnosis, some stage hypnotists do try it out on an audience before a show in order to see how susceptible people are to the power of suggestion.

1 Ask the spectators to interlock their fingers and hold their first fingers out in front of them. They must separate their fingertips as much as possible. Explain that you are going to hypnotize them, and tell them a story about very strong magnets being implanted in the tips of their fingers, drawing their fingertips closer together until they lock together. You could also mime binding people's fingers together with invisible thread.

2 Believe it or not, the spectators will find they can do nothing to resist their fingers getting closer together until they touch. Why does this work? The fingers are being stretched apart at the beginning and after a few moments muscle fatigue sets in and the muscles have to contract.

wand twist

The challenge is to copy the trickster with a simple move that seems easy to replicate. However, unless they know the secret few will be

able to succeed. Make it clear at the beginning that they are not allowed to let go of the wand or stick at any time.

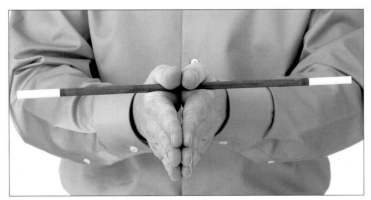

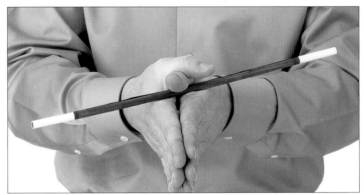

1 With your hands held palm to palm, hold a magic wand, pencil or other stick-like object with your thumbs as shown.

2 Cross your thumbs, right over left. This will make the wand start to twist to the right.

3 The right hand turns downward and the left upward, palms wiping against each other. The stick remains between the thumbs.

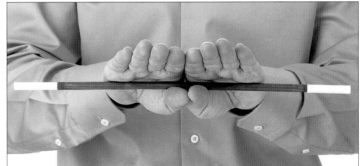

4 Carry on turning the hands until the palms are facing the floor. When these moves are all put together the crossing of the thumbs goes unnoticed and people will get themselves into a muddle, ending up with their hands pointing in opposite directions.

floating arms

This weird stunt is something I used to do all the time as a teenager. It is very effective and creates a really strange sensation. As with *many of the stunts in this chapter, you have to try it yourself in order to realize how odd the experience is.*

1 Stand behind someone and hold their arms to their sides. They must push their arms outwards for about 45 seconds.

2 When you let go, the other person's arms will rise upwards as if they are being pulled up by invisible strings.

pepper-sepper-ation

A small quantity of pepper is sprinkled on to the surface of a glass of water. The trickster touches the water with the tip of a toothpick and *the pepper reacts by moving away from the toothpick in the most dramatic way. When anyone else tries to copy the stunt, it won't work.*

secret view

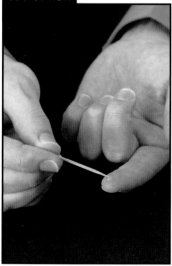

1 Coat the tip of a toothpick with a dot of liquid soap.

2 Sprinkle some pepper into a glass of water.

3 There should be enough pepper to cover the surface. Now touch the tip of the toothpick to the centre of the surface of the water.

4 Watch as the pepper jumps away from the toothpick. Remove the toothpick from the water and wipe the end dry, removing all traces of soap as you do so. When someone else tries the trick, either with the same or a different toothpick, it won't work.

tip *Use a pen instead of a toothpick. If you keep a tiny piece of sponge soaked in washing-up liquid in the cap of the pen it will be ready to work at any moment. In fact, when you put the lid on the pen to put it away, it will recoat itself for your next performance.*

table lock

If you really want to make a friend look silly, try this the next time you are out for a drink. Be prepared to make a hasty exit!

Ask your friend to place both hands palm down, flat on the table. Now take two full glasses and carefully balance them on the backs of your friend's hands. They will now be unable to move their hands without the glasses falling and the drinks spilling everywhere. This is a good time for you and your other friends to walk away and leave your victim sitting alone in this rather awkward predicament!

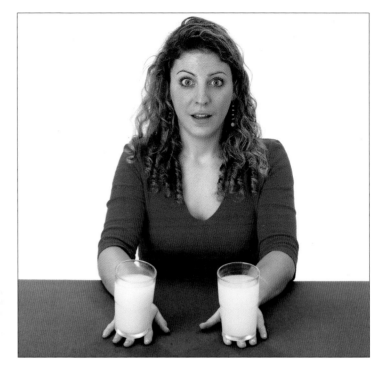

tip *Is is not advisable to perform this stunt on a surface that could be damaged by the spilled drinks.*

broom suspension

This cheeky trick leaves your victim left high but not necessarily dry. Only try it in suitable surroundings and never without the *permission of the person who lives there. It is especially funny when you trick somebody who is a bit of a know-all or show off.*

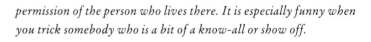

1 You will need a plastic cup (it must be plastic, never glass) full of water and a long stick. A broom handle is perfect but a snooker cue might also do the job. Stand your victim up and ask them to hold the stick in the air. Now climb on a chair and trap the plastic cup between the end of the stick and the ceiling.

2 That's all there is to it: you can just walk away or continue your conversation some distance away and your victim will be stuck wondering how to move without getting soaked. If they find a way to do it, let me know!

time for a shower

This party challenge could result in someone getting very wet, so you should only attempt it in an area that can easily be cleaned and won't *be damaged by liquid being spilled. You may have to practise the stunt a few times before you get it right.*

1 Place a plate over a glass full of liquid. Here we have used coloured liquid so you can see what is happening.

2 Hold the glass firmly to the plate and turn everything over. Put it back on the table. The challenge is to drink the liquid inside the glass, but you are allowed to use only one hand.

3 The secret to achieving this is to hold the plate and push your forehead firmly against the base of the glass.

4 Now slowly and carefully stand upright and make sure the glass is balanced properly.

5 Once the glass is vertical and balanced, remove the plate.

6 Now you can put the plate down and lift the glass from your forehead, leaving you in a position to drink the liquid normally.

inverted glass trick

In another funny stunt you turn a glass of liquid upside down, without the liquid leaking out. It is now impossible to turn the *glass the right way without the liquid spilling and making a mess. Only perform this stunt on a suitable surface.*

1 Cover a glass of liquid with a piece of card (stock). Here, we have used coloured liquid so you can see what is happening, but it can be anything.

2 Quickly turn everything upside down, holding the card firmly against the mouth of the glass to stop any of the liquid escaping.

3 Place the glass and the card upside down on a table.

4 Slide out the card and the glass will remain full, but upside down. It is now impossible to move the glass without creating a complete mess, so don't try this in the dining room or in someone else's home without their permission.

coin through hole

The challenge is to push a large coin through a hole only half its size. The paper can be folded but not torn. Allow spectators to have a go at doing it themselves before you show them how it is done. Unless they have seen the stunt before, they won't be able to do it.

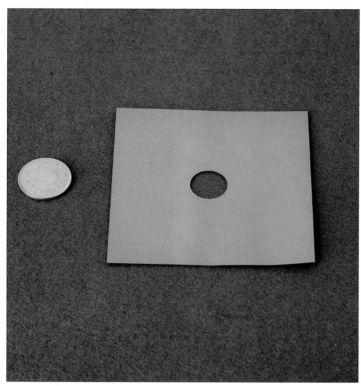

1 Carefully cut a hole about 1.5cm (⅝in) in diameter in a piece of paper. You will also need a coin that is clearly considerably larger than the hole.

2 Fold the piece of paper in half, with the hole facing down, towards the table.

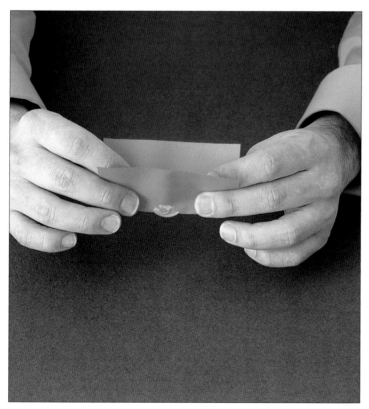

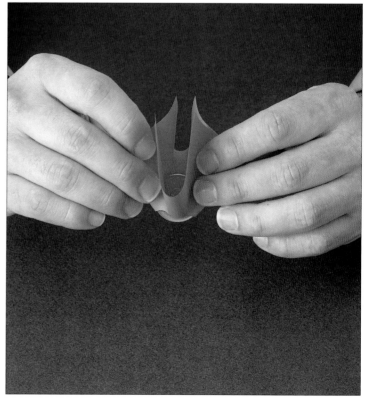

3 Drop the coin into the folded piece of paper so that it rests in the hole.

4 Now bend the paper upwards as shown. This action will stretch the hole.

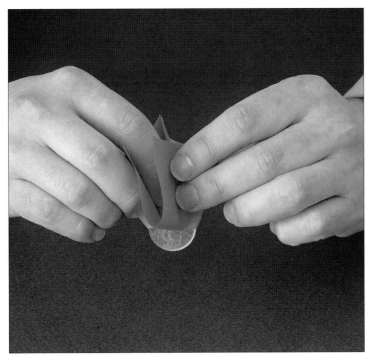

5 This allows you to push the coin carefully through the hole without damaging the paper.

6 You may need to experiment with holes and coins of different sizes in order to create the best-looking illusion possible.

rising tube mystery

A paper tube held together with paperclips is seen threaded on to two lengths of cord. Defying gravity, the tube not only remains suspended when held upright, but rises up the cords in an uncanny fashion. Everything is handed out for examination.

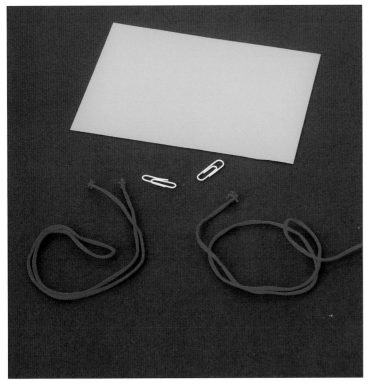

1 You will need a sheet of paper, two paperclips and two identical, long pieces of cord.

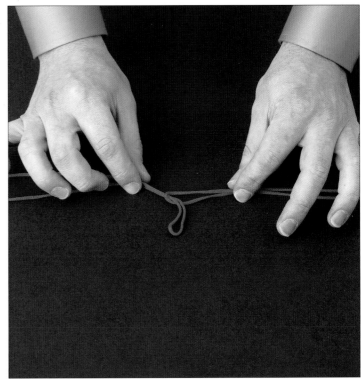

2 Fold both lengths of cord in half and insert the centre of one through the other to create a small loop. ▶

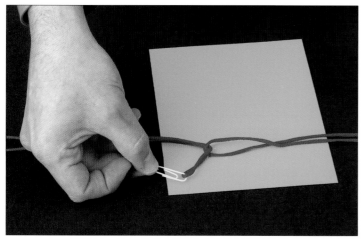

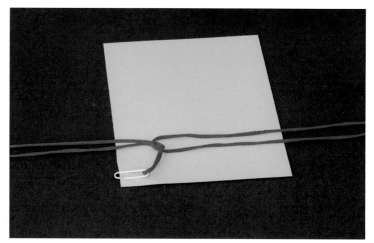

3 Attach a paperclip to the loop and clip this on to the edge of the paper.

4 If you have attached it properly, the set up should now look like this, and everything should be secure.

5 Now roll up the paper into a tight tube so that the cord is on the inside.

6 Once the whole sheet is rolled, reposition the paperclip so that it holds the roll together.

7 Use a second paperclip to hold the roll securely at the other end. This one should be clipped only to the paper and not to the cords.

8 To complete the set-up, pull on the cords until the loop is just at the top of the tube.

9 Hold the cords up by the end and show that the tube is defying gravity.

10 Grip the bottom cords and pull very gently.

11 The tube will slowly travel up the cords!

12 When the tube reaches the top, hold both ends of the cords together and begin to disassemble the cords from the paper.

13 Remove both paperclips and show them to the audience.

14 Unroll the paper and hand everything out to the audience for examination. You could even challenge them to try to do it themselves!

suspended animation

A mug dropped from a height is expected to hit the floor and shatter, but instead it stops short and remains suspended in the air. As with *many stunts, science plays a key role, enabling you to harness the laws of physics and perform an extraordinary feat.*

1 Prepare by tapping a nail into the side of a pencil.

2 Tie one end of a long piece of cord to the handle of a mug and the other end to a washer.

3 Hold the washer in one hand and the pencil in the other. The cord hangs over the pencil.

4 This close-up view shows how the string sits alongside the nail.

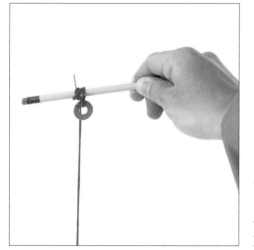

5 The cord is released and the mug plunges towards the floor.

6 Amazingly, the cord winds itself around the pencil, stopping the mug from hitting the floor and breaking.

7 This close-up view shows how the weight of the washer has stopped the cord from unwinding and the nail helps to stop the cord from slipping.

straw bottle

The challenge is to pick up a bottle with a straw. There are several ways you can achive this, including tying the straw around the neck of the bottle, but the solution shown below is more fun and less obvious and, therefore, more impressive.

1 Display a bottle and challenge the spectators to lift it from the table using just a drinking straw.

2 The solution is simple. Bend the straw about one-third of the way up and then insert it into the bottle. The fold in the straw will spring open inside, and it will lock into place, enabling you to lift the bottle off the table.

escaping coin

A conical glass has a small coin at the bottom of the glass covered by a large coin on top of it. How do you remove the small coin without touching either the glass or the coins? This may require several attempts, but you will be able to do it in the end.

1 You will need a conical glass, a large coin and a tiny coin.

2 Drop the smallest coin into the conical glass.

3 Drop the larger coin on top of it, so that it covers the smaller coin.

4 Blow sharply into the near side of the glass, in the direction shown by the arrow.

5 Believe it or not the larger coin will flip out of the way and the small coin will fly out of the glass.

balancing skill

Two forks are suspended from the top of a bottle on the tip of a match in an amazing display of balance. Ask members of your audience to *have a go for themselves before you show them how it is done. It is very unlikely that they will be able to do it.*

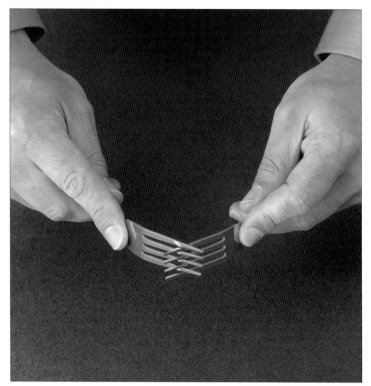

1 Give the audience enough time to try this out for themselves, then lock the prongs of two forks together.

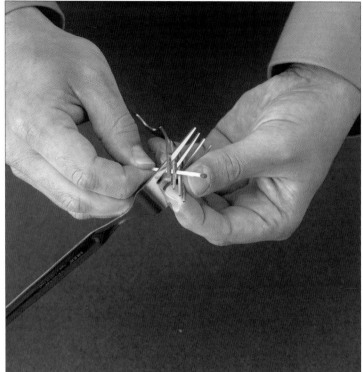

2 Insert a match through the middle, between the prongs so that it joins them together, as shown.

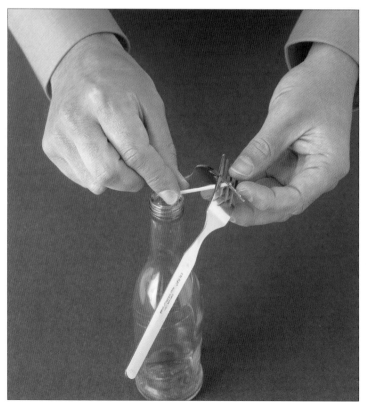

3 Carefully balance the tip of the match (the non-striking end) on the rim of a bottle. You may need to adjust things until you find the centre of balance.

4 Once you have balanced the match and forks properly you can walk away and allow the audience to come and have a closer look at how you have achieved this feat.

card flick

Have you ever seen a tablecloth whipped off a table, leaving all the glasses and cutlery in place? This is a scaled-down version and is considerably easier to achieve after a little practice, although no less impressive than the larger scale version.

1 Begin by balancing a coin on top of a playing card on the tip of your finger.

2 Get ready to flick the card away from you.

3 If you are quick, the card will shoot out from under the coin, leaving it neatly on the tip of your finger.

the rice lift

How do you lift a jar of uncooked rice with a single chopstick? You can also use a pencil or knife in place of the chopstick. Other types of container can be used but the important factor is the shape: the container must have a "shoulder" below the neck.

3 When you can physically feel the resistance, give the chopstick one last push all the way down to the bottom of the jar and then lift the jar slowly from the table.

1 Fill a jar with short grain, uncooked rice. Put the lid on the jar and bang on the table to pack the rice down as far as possible. Remove the lid and push the chopstick down into the rice.

2 Work the chopstick up and down 30–50 times. This motion will pack the rice tightly against the sides of the jar. The more you "stab" the rice the harder it will become to pull the chopstick free.

Robin Hood meets his match

Your friends will credit you with the skill of Robin Hood when you demonstrate this clever stunt. It is not quite as difficult as it seems but looks mighty impressive. You may need to start off quite close to *the target until you get used to the trick. Once you are good at it you can begin to increase the distance between your hand and the matchbox, which will make it look even more impressive.*

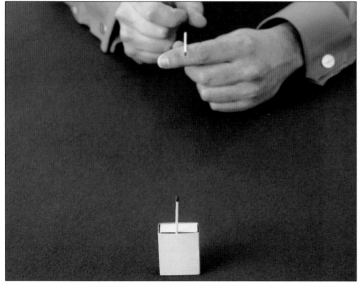

1 Remove two matches from the box and carefully trap one in the drawer. Only the bottom of the matchstick should be caught in the box. Set the box about 30cm (12in) away from you and balance the other match on your left forefinger and thumb.

2 Flick the match off your finger with your right hand and you will knock the other match out of the box. The reason for this is that the match will spin and turn sideways as it leaves your left hand, but it happens so fast that no one can see how it works.

immovable

As a demonstration of your superhuman strength, you touch your first fingers together at the tips and challenge someone to pull them apart. *Nobody can do it! You could combine this trick with Move My Fists or Try and Stand Up as they work nicely together.*

Touch your fingertips together, holding your arms as shown. As long as your challenger holds your wrists they will fail to move your fingertips apart. Their energy is dissipated and leaves your fingers unaffected.

tip *These stunts look especially impressive when the challenger is a child or someone who is smaller and clearly weaker than the person they are challenging.*

try and stand up!

You prove you are incredibly strong by stopping someone from standing up using just one finger. This effective trick is particularly *funny when a child pins a parent or other adult to their chair, and it can easily be incorporated into any show.*

Ask someone to sit down on a chair and hold your first finger against their forehead. Tell them they are not allowed to remove your finger. They now have to try to stand up. They won't be able to do it because their centre of balance is above their lap and they can't move their head forward to compensate for that.

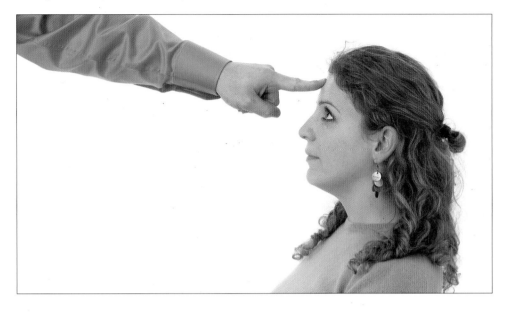

surefire bet

Ask someone to stand with their back to the wall. You place a large denomination banknote in front of their feet and explain that they *can keep the note if they can pick it up without losing contact with the wall. They will be unable to do it, and you will keep the money.*

1 When you position the person ensure their heels are touching the wall. Explain that their heels must not lose contact with the wall. Place the banknote just in front of their feet.

2 They will be unable to pick up the note without losing their balance. Shifting their centre of gravity causes them to fall away from the wall, and there is nothing they can do about it.

lift me if you can

How is it possible to drain someone of their strength in a split second? Easy, just read on! It is even more impressive if you train a small child to do this stunt so that they can flummox an adult.

1 Stand with your arms folded up and your elbows locked in to your sides.

2 Get someone to lift you off the ground holding you by your elbows. In this position it is relatively easy.

3 When you want to create the illusion of making the person seem instantly weak, simply move your elbows out to the position shown. It is a subtle difference but one that really matters.

4 Now it is impossible for them to raise you off the ground at all, because moving the elbows out has shifted the centre of gravity.

superman

In yet another demonstration of your superhuman strength, you hold a broomstick or a pole in both hands and challenge anyone to push you off your spot. Nobody, no matter how big and strong they are, will be able to do it.

1 Hold a broom handle or other long stick with both hands and ensure that your feet are shoulder-width apart and your elbows are bent. Your challenger takes hold of the broom with both hands outside yours and try as they might they cannot push you off the spot.

2 This stunt also works if you hold the ends of the broom and they place their hands in the middle. Bending your arms simply dissipates all the energy that is being thrown at you.

box it

Match puzzles have been in existence for almost as long as matches themselves, and they are particularly good since they can be performed anywhere. This puzzle is a classic and is not too difficult. The challenge is to move just two matches to make six squares.

1 Lay 12 matches on the table to form four squares.

2 Pick up the middle left match and position to bisect the top left square.

tip *You could also use pencils, chopsticks, toothpicks or any other straight objects that you have to hand to perform these simple match puzzles.*

3 Move the bottom middle match and place it at 90 degrees to the other match to form a square within a square.

numbers up

You are not allowed to break any matches to solve this puzzle. The secret to finding the answer is to think laterally. You may need to drop hints for those of your friends who are finding it hard to solve the puzzle for themselves.

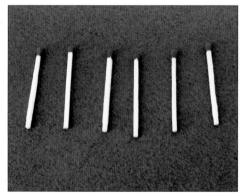

1 Rearrange these six matches to make the number twenty-five.

2 This configuration makes 25 in Roman numerals!

fish!

Can you make this fish swim in the opposite direction in just three moves? Even when you know the solution to this puzzle, it is quite *difficult to get right. It is worth trying it yourself and practising if necessary before challenging someone else to do it.*

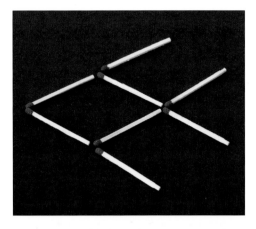

1 Use eight matches to make the image of a fish.

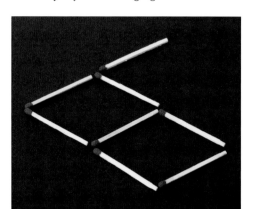

2 Move the top far right match and position as shown here.

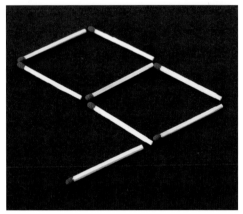

3 Move the top right match and place it at the bottom on the left, as shown.

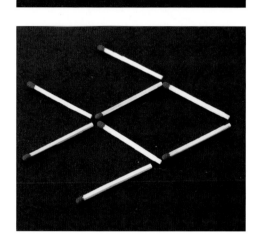

4 Finally, move the top left match and position as shown.

cocktail glass

Can you work out how to remove the cherry from the glass by moving just two matches? The glass must not change shape. *The reason that this puzzle is so hard to solve is due to the fact that the glass ends up at a different angle from that at which it started.*

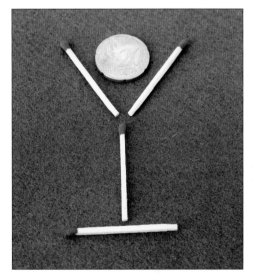

1 Lay four matches in the shape of a cocktail glass and put a coin in the glass to represent a cherry.

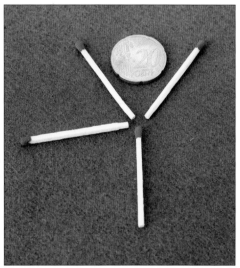

2 Move the bottom match and position as shown.

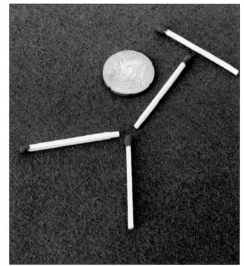

3 Move the match to the left of the coin as shown. The glass has rotated but did not change shape!

uncrushable!

In this interesting demonstration you show an audience how to make the drawer of a matchbox virtually uncrushable. Experiment using *matchboxes of different sizes and types, as these factors may affect how well the stunt works.*

1 If you place the drawer of a matchbox on top of the cover and bang your fist down, both parts will be damaged. However, if you place the cover on top and try the same thing you won't be able to crush the drawer.

2 Try it! The drawer will spring away from you and remain undamaged.

suspension bridge

The challenge here is to find a way to suspend the middle glass between the outer two, using only the banknote for support. *The two outer glasses must not move. The solution involves a little origami in order to increase the strength of the paper.*

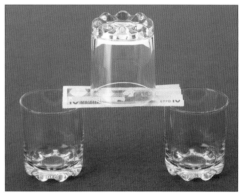

1 Gather together a crisp banknote and three glasses. Position the glasses close together in a row.

2 Pleat the note horizontally, using as many small folds as possible, making sure each crease is as firm as possible.

3 Now place the note between the two glasses and you will find it is strong enough to hold the third glass. Note how the third glass has been turned over so that the weight is distributed over a larger area.

coin con

In this stunt you have to remove the paper the coins are resting on, but leave the coins in place balanced on the rims of the glasses. *This stunt uses the same method as that which was used for Card Flick and may require a few goes in order for it to work properly.*

1 Place two coins on a slip of paper resting on two glasses.

2 Simply strike the paper firmly with your finger, in the centre and straight down to the table. The speed of the movement will free the paper and leave both coins sitting on the edge of the glasses, undisturbed.

the pyramid game

Can you turn the pyramid upside down by moving only three coins? Many people have access to enough coins for this puzzle, whether *ones that they happen to have in their pocket or that are borrowed from friends, making this a great impromptu trick.*

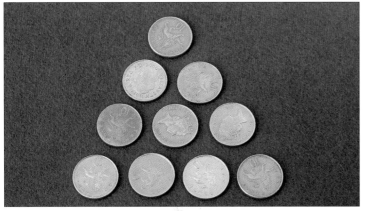

1 Lay ten coins, preferably of the same denomination, on a table in a pyramid shape.

2 Pick up the coin at the bottom right of the triangle and position as shown here.

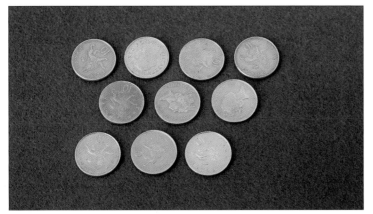

3 Move the coin at the top of the triangle and put it at the end left of the top row.

4 Move the bottom left coin and position so that it completes the upside down triangle.

riddle me this

Ask your friends this riddle and see if they can work out which card is where. This simple conundrum is particularly good when you pose *it at a party or other social occasion where a group may not know each other, as it will get people talking.*

1 The riddle is: "To the left of a Club is a King.
To the right of a King is an Eight.
The Diamond is not the Four or next to the Four.
Home is where the heart is."

2 And here is the answer. Did you get it right? Now try challenging friends and family to solve it.

letter of resignation

Can you draw the design in step 5 without taking your pen off the paper and without going over any line twice? Even though there are only a limited number of ways this can be attempted, it is surprising how long it takes to work it out.

1 Start at the bottom right corner and smoothly draw the shape shown.

2 Continue to draw, as shown, making sure the pen doesn't leave the paper.

3 Complete the outside of the shape as shown in the picture.

4 Finally, complete the cross in the middle of the box. Practise a few times before you try to challenge anyone else to do it.

5 When you try this out on someone else you will need to show them a picture of the final design, so make sure that you have one to hand before you begin.

bullseye

Or try this puzzle – can you draw a dot in the centre of a circle without taking your pen off the paper? This is possible, but only *if you cheat a little, which will both infuriate and amuse the people who you challenge to solve the puzzle.*

1 Loosely fold over the top corner of a piece of paper. Make a dot where the corner meets the page.

2 Now run the pen across the folded corner and back on to the front of the sheet.

3 Allow the paper to unfold and draw the circle around the central dot.

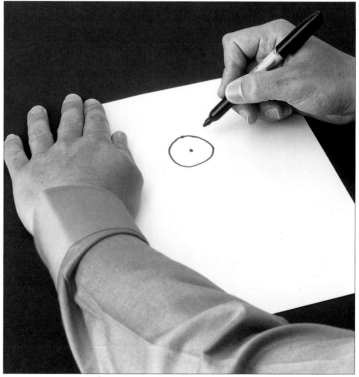

4 This completes the picture. You are now ready to challenge someone else to try and do it.

total this sum

This is the perfect puzzle to show a maths teacher or accountant. Try it yourself and see how deceptive it is. Simply add up the numbers listed below. If you get a total of 5,000 then you are wrong and you will need to try again.

Write down the following numbers: 1,000; 40; 1,000; 30; 1,000; 20; 1,000; 10. Add them up and see what total you get.

tip *The reason that people get a total of 5,000 is because they begin to count in a rhythm that makes them incorrectly anticipate what the answer is.*

impossible numbers!

Write down the following number on a piece of paper as quickly as possible: eleven thousand, eleven hundred and eleven. Tricky, isn't it! Now try asking your friends and family to have a go – you will be amazed how few people get it right first time.

1 Did you write down 11,1111? If so then you are incorrect and should try again.

2 The reason this is so difficult to write is because of the way the number is said. "Eleven hundred" is, of course, one thousand, one hundred, but most people write a string of ones in an attempt to write it as quickly as possible.

calculation sensation

Someone thinks of any number between 1 and 63. With the aid of six cards (each with a huge list of numbers on it) the magician can reveal *what the number was that the spectator thought of. It is one of the oldest mathematical puzzles, and is still very effective.*

1 Use a computer to make the six cards you will use for the calculation. These are the numbers you should type on each:

Card 1: 1 3 5 7 9 11 13 15 17 19 21 23 25 27 29 31 33 35 37 39 41 43 45 47 49 51 53 55 57 59 61

Card 2: 2 3 6 7 10 11 14 15 18 19 22 23 26 27 30 31 34 35 38 39 42 43 46 47 50 51 54 55 58 59 62 63

Card 3: 4 5 6 7 12 13 14 15 20 21 22 23 28 29 30 31 36 37 38 39 44 45 46 47 52 53 54 55 60 61 62 63

Card 4: 8 9 10 11 12 13 14 15 24 25 26 27 28 29 30 31 40 41 42 43 44 45 46 47 56 57 58 59 60 61 62 63

Card 5: 16 17 18 19 20 21 22 23 24 25 26 27 28 29 30 31 48 49 50 51 52 53 54 55 56 57 58 59 60 61 62 63

Card 6: 32 33 34 35 36 37 38 39 40 41 42 43 44 45 46 47 48 49 50 51 52 53 54 55 56 57 58 59 60 61 62 63

As long as you keep these groups of numbers together you can make cards of any shape you like. Just make sure the first number is always top left.

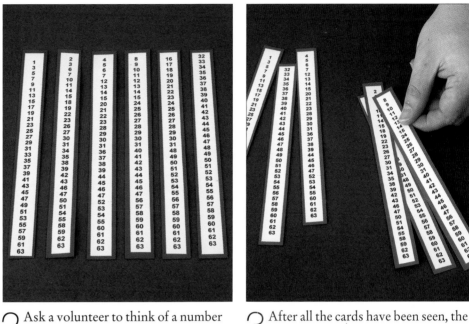

2 Ask a volunteer to think of a number between 1 and 63. Show them the cards in any order and ask them to tell you if their number appears upon it. If it does, remember the top number. Continue showing the cards, asking the same question each time. Each time they say "yes", add the number at the top of the card, keeping a running total in your head.

3 After all the cards have been seen, the total in your head is the number that the person is thinking of. In this example that number is 37.

hide and seek

While your back is turned an object is placed under one of three mugs. When you turn around you are able to pick the correct mug every single time. This trick requires a stooge or confederate, whom *no one will suspect. You must be sure not to glance at your helper in an obvious way. The trick will keep spectators baffled for a long time as long as you are both subtle.*

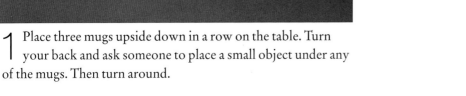

1 Place three mugs upside down in a row on the table. Turn your back and ask someone to place a small object under any of the mugs. Then turn around.

2 Your confederate watches carefully and indicates the correct mug by holding up the relevant number of fingers. In this example the object is under the third mug.

hide and seek solo

While your back is turned an object is placed under one of three mugs and the position of the two empty mugs is switched. When you turn around you know where the object is. You can repeat this trick again and again. It will fool even the brightest people.

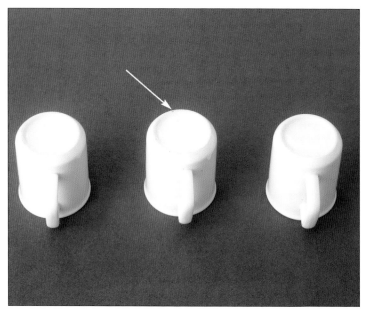

1 You will need three opaque cups or mugs, of which one must have an identifying feature on its base. Any tiny mark or blemish that you will recognize will work. Put the three mugs upside down in a row, with the marked mug in the centre.

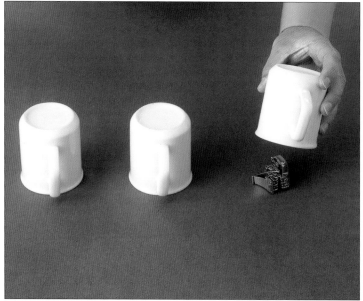

2 Turn your back and instruct someone to place an object such as a coin or watch under any mug.

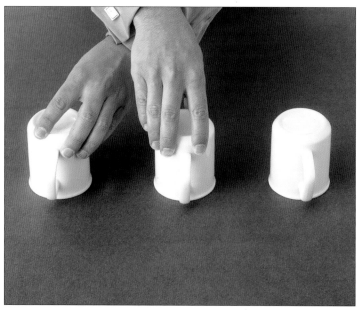

3 Tell the volunteer to switch the positions of the two empty mugs while your back is turned.

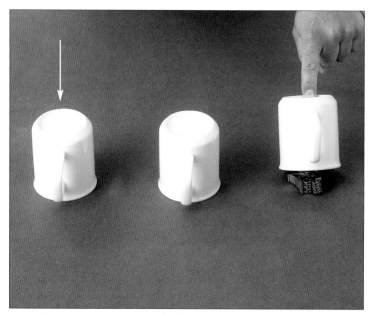

4 When you turn around, look for the marked mug. If it is still in the middle, that is where the object must be. If the marked mug is now at one end of the row, the object will be under the cup at the opposite end.

tip *You may find that borrowed mugs already have small identifying features, such as chips or scratches, if you look closely enough. If you want to use your own cups it is easy to mark one of them, but be sure to make it subtle.*

topsy-turvy mugs

In this classic puzzle you line up three mugs with one upside down, then by turning two mugs at a time you manage to get all three the *right way up in just three moves. When you challenge others to do the same, they just won't be able to do it. Why not? Because you cheat!*

1 Line up three mugs, placing the mug at each end mouth down and the centre mug mouth up. This is the starting position for the puzzle.

2 Pick up the left-hand mug and the centre mug. In one swift movement turn both mugs over and place them back where they were. This is move 1.

3 Now pick up the end mugs. Once again turn them both over and replace them where they came from. This is move 2.

4 Finally turn over the left hand mug and the centre mug (repeating move 1). This third and final move will result in all three mugs being mouth up.

5 Turn over the centre mug and challenge a spectator to do what you just did. Here is the sneaky bit; the mugs are in fact now laid out in the exact opposite to the way it was when you did it. The spectators won't notice this small change and will be baffled as to how you managed to get all three mugs facing up in just three moves.

x-ray vision

While your back is turned a coin is placed under a mug. When you turn around you are able to determine what denomination of coin it is. This trick also requires a stooge or confederate, which means that you must teach it to a friend, who will be your secret helper when you perform it. The two of you need to practise the trick a lot so that you can get it right every time.

1 The handle of the mug can be turned to point in any direction. Take one coin of each denomination used in your currency and lay them out around the mug like a clock. Put the lowest denomination at the 1 o'clock position, with the others equally spaced. This photograph shows British currency, which has eight different coins.

2 In performance you ask someone to place any coin on the table while your back is turned. Then you ask for the coin to be covered with the mug. This is when your friend picks up the mug and positions it so that the handle points in the correct direction for that coin. If you both always assume that the 12 o'clock position is where your friend is standing you will always get the orientation of the mug correct. Which coin do you think is under the mug in this example?

3 It was the 20 pence coin. Did you get it right?

penny pincher

The challenge is to remove both coins balanced on a glass at the same time, with one hand and without making direct contact with the glass. This may require some practice but you will soon be able to perform it perfectly every time.

1 Balance two coins on the rim of a glass, arranging them on opposite sides, as shown here.

2 Place the tip of your thumb on one coin and the tip of your forefinger on the other coin.

3 Drag the coins on to the outside of the glass, being careful not to touch the glass with your hand or fingers.

4 Now raise your hand quickly, pinching your finger and thumb together. The coins will momentarily stick to your fingertips and you can remove both coins together.

the great olive challenge

How can you move an olive from a table to a cocktail glass without the olive ever touching your hands? The shape of the glasses is important, but since both types can often be found in bars and restaurants, this is a perfect stunt for either location.

1 As well as the cocktail glass and the olive you will need a second, tulip-shaped glass.

2 Pick up the second glass and invert it over the olive.

3 Spin the glass around so that centrifugal force keeps the olive whizzing around the inside of the glass.

4 Without stopping, move it over the top of the cocktail glass.

5 Slowly bring the glass to a halt and allow the olive to drop into the glass below.

invisible traveller

In this deceptive puzzle you cause a single card to travel from one place to another while everything is in the spectator's hands. This is also *known as the Piano Trick. With a bit of thought you could replace the playing cards with other objects that could make a fun presentation.*

1 Begin with a deck of cards positioned in front of you. Ask a volunteer to place their hands flat on the table, palms down, as shown.

2 Pick up two cards from the top of the pile and say, "Two cards are even."

3 Place this pair between the fourth and third fingers of the person's right hand. Now pick up two more cards and say again, "Two cards are even." Place these between the third and second fingers of the right hand.

4 Repeat this again and again on both hands until you reach the final space that is left between the left hand's third and fourth fingers, where you place only one card and say: "One card is odd."

5 Pick up the first pair you dealt and split them, starting two piles on the table. As you lay the pair of cards down on the table say: "Even."

6 Repeat this dealing process, taking each pair and saying "Even" as you lay them on the piles, until you have a single card remaining. Ask the person which pile they would like the odd card to be placed on. Put the last card down on the pile they point to.

7 Make a mystic pass over the two piles and explain that you are invisibly transferring the odd card from one pile to the other. You now count out the piles and it is seen that the pile containing an odd number of cards is the opposite pile to the one chosen for the odd card to be placed on! Really, nothing has happened. The fact is, before the single card was added to a pile in step 6 both piles contained an odd number of cards: because you split the pairs into two piles of seven cards. Your patter has created the impression that both piles are even and that is what makes the trick work.

the trapdoor card

This superb puzzle is the brainchild of Robert Neale, from the USA. There have been many versions of this trick over the years. I use a version in my professional work as it is absolutely baffling and one of the very best puzzles you can learn. Do not underestimate the effect it will have on spectators. Thanks to Robert for allowing me to share his idea with you.

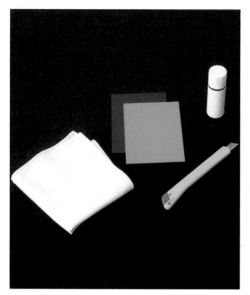

1 You will need some adhesive glue, a handkerchief, a craft knife and two pieces of card (stock) approximately 12.5 x 7.5cm (5 x 3in) in different colours (we used green and red in this example).

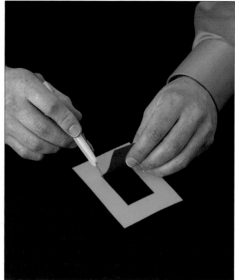

2 Glue the coloured cards together back to back then cut a trapdoor in the card. You should cut three sides, leaving one of the short ends intact for the hinge. The border should be about 2cm (¾in) wide. Crease the hinge sharply.

3 With the red side upwards, ask someone to hold on to the trapdoor. Notice that the opening is facing away from them.

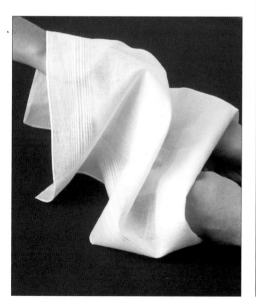

4 Explain that you are going to turn the card over, even though they will not let go of the card or turn their hand over. It doesn't sound possible. To keep the secret, throw a handkerchief over their hand and the card.

secret view

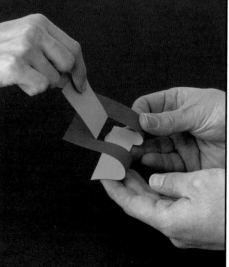

5 The handkerchief has been removed in these pictures so you can see what is happening, but you must leave it in position while you make these moves. First, bend the end of the card underneath.

secret view

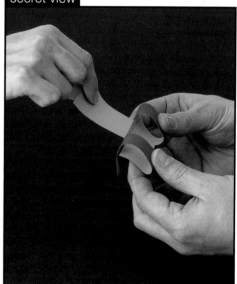

6 Now roll the top underneath so that the folds overlap.

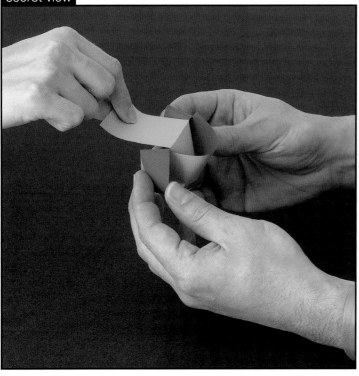

7 Roll the sides of the card back and bring them through the hole in the middle.

8 As you do this, the card will slowly begin to turn inside out. Do not rush this movement or you may tear the card.

9 Carefully pull the rolled edges all the way through the hole and open them out.

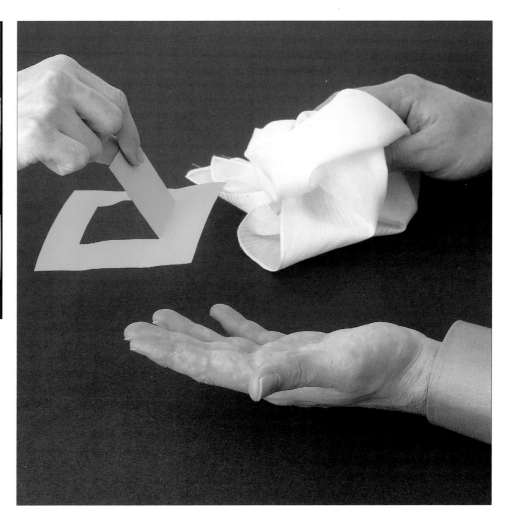

10 Now remove the handkerchief and show that the card is now upside down!

walking through a postcard

Give someone a postcard and a pair of scissors, and tell them it is possible to cut a hole in the card big enough for you to step through.

See if they can figure out how. Unless they know the secret it is unlikely they will succeed.

1 Fold the postcard in half lengthwise. You can use a plain card, or one with a picture on it.

2 Make straight cuts in from the folded edge approximately every 1cm (½in). Notice how each cut stops approximately 1cm (½in) short of the opposite edge.

3 Turn the card round and cut more slits (marked here in red) between the slits you have already made, this time starting from the open edges rather than the fold. These slits stop 1cm (½in) from the folded edge, as before.

4 Now trim off about 3mm (⅛in) along the fold, except for the sections at each end.

5 When you open up the card you will find it now has a hole in it large enough for you to step through.

6 If you want to show this stunt but don't have a postcard with you, you can use a business card or playing card instead, with the challenge: "Cut a hole big enough for me to put my head through."

drink problem

How can you drink from an unopened bottle? Next time you are at a table where there is an unopened bottle of wine or mineral water, try *challenging your companions. You will need to have some wine or water already poured in a glass.*

1 Show an unopened bottle of wine or water and pose the problem.

2 Turn the bottle upside down and pour some wine or water from your glass into the dimple at the bottom.

3 Now take a sip from the dimple and you have shown how to drink from the unopened bottle!

a cutting problem

The solution to this simple puzzle requires a little lateral thinking, and the solution is guaranteed to make your audience groan. *It would work very well as part of an act in conjunction with Suspended Animation since both use the same props.*

1 Tie a piece of string to the handle of a mug and hold it up high. The challenge is to cut the string between the handle and your hand without the mug falling.

2 Tie a medium-size loop in the piece of string.

3 Snip through the loop and the mug will stay where it is!

salt and pepper separation

How can you sort out a mixture of salt and pepper? This stunt makes use of static electricity to cause the particles of pepper to separate *instantly from a pile of salt, and demonstrates once again how you can harness the laws of science to perform fun stunts.*

1 Pour a quantity of salt on to a surface, which should preferably be dark so that you can see what is happening clearly.

2 Now sprinkle some powdered pepper on top of the pile of salt on the paper.

3 Rub a balloon on your hair to create a static charge and hold the balloon just above the pile of salt and pepper. The pepper will jump up and cling to the surface of the balloon while the salt stays on the table.

tip *You can use a plastic comb instead of a balloon, if you prefer. Simply run the comb through your hair a few times, then position the teeth close to the salt and pepper mixture. Try to use a white comb if you can, so that you can see the particles of pepper clearly.*

crazy corks

You make a simple move with two corks and ask the spectators to copy you. While you can make the move with ease, they will get *themselves in a tangle. The corks in the photographs have red dots on one end and you should do the same to make the trick easy to follow.*

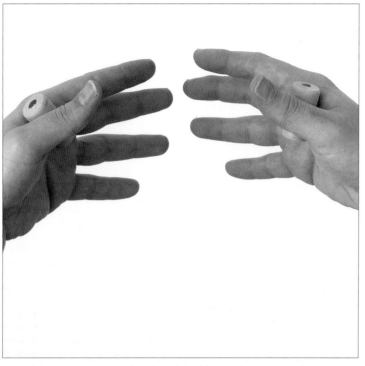

1 Pick up a cork in either hand, holding it in the crotch of the thumb as shown.

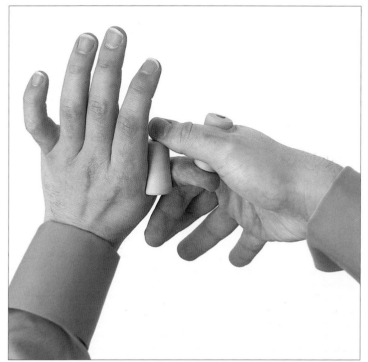

2 Turn your left wrist back towards you so that you can place the thumbs of both hands on the ends of the corks that do not have spots.

3 Now place the first finger of each hand on the ends of the corks that do have spots.

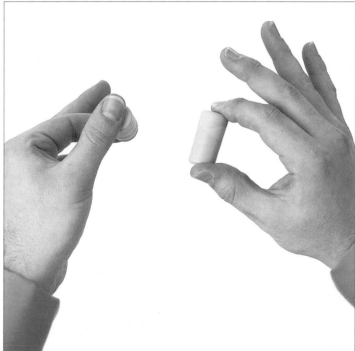

4 Untwist your left hand from your right and the two corks will be separated. Of course, they were never really linked but when others try to copy your moves they will find themselves in a muddle.

quickness of the hand

Have you heard the expression, "The quickness of the hand deceives the eye"? This little stunt proves the exact opposite. You see the money fall but you can't close your hand fast enough. This surely proves the eye is quicker than the hand.*

1 Hold a banknote at the very top and ask someone to hold their finger and thumb open, ready to catch it. The idea is simple: you will drop the money and if they catch it they can keep it! Don't worry: your money is safe, as long as you ensure their fingers are open and halfway up the banknote.

2 Their natural response will be too slow. The only way they will catch it is if they guess when you are going to drop it.

love match

The challenge here is to remove a coin without the matches that are balanced on it falling. The trick gets its title because the two matches look as if they are kissing. Whenever you handle matches you should exercise great care, and children must always be supervized by an adult.*

1 Remove two matches from the box and, working on a plate, carefully trap one in the drawer. Rest the other match on a coin and balance it against the head of the first one.

2 In order to do this you will need another box of matches or a lighter. Ignite the heads of the balanced matches.

3 Wait a few seconds and the head of the match resting on the coin will fuse to the other and curl upwards. Blow out the matches and pick up the coin.

interlocked

Two people have their wrists tied together with rope. The ropes are interlocked and the challenge is for the two to separate without untying the knots. Unless they know the secret, this problem can take a long time to solve.

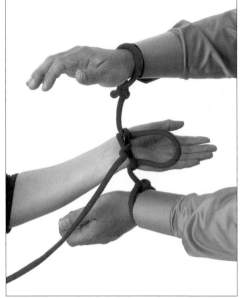

1 Tie a length of rope around both wrists of each of two people. Before you make the last knot, link the two ropes as shown.

2 To get free, one person must thread the centre of their rope under the loop around one of the other person's wrists.

3 This loop is then slipped over the top of their hand.

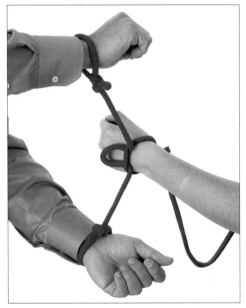

4 The back view shows how the ropes are being untangled.

5 The result is that the two people have released one another without untying the knots.

impossible link

A pencil on a loop of string is attached to someone's buttonhole. While you seemed to put it on easily they will have a tough time getting the *pencil off again unless they know the secret. This is a fantastic stunt to play on people, and is guaranteed to frustrate them.*

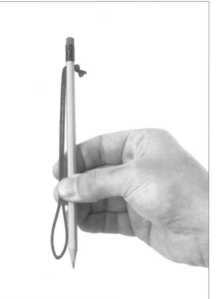

1 Pencils with string attached can sometimes be found in novelty and souvenir shops but are hard to find. It is easy to make your own by drilling a small hole in the top of a pencil and then tying a loop of string through the hole.

2 The loop of string must be a little shorter than the pencil (even when stretched to its full extent).

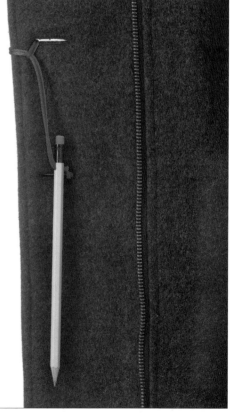

3 Pull a large section of the coat near a buttonhole through the loop of the string. You need to pull as much material through the loop as possible.

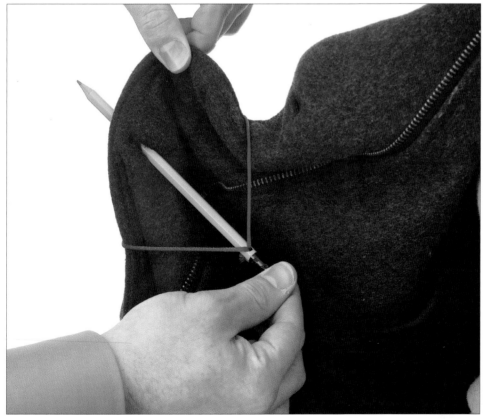

4 Carefully guide the tip of the pencil through the buttonhole of the coat. You may need to use a bit of force to get the angle right.

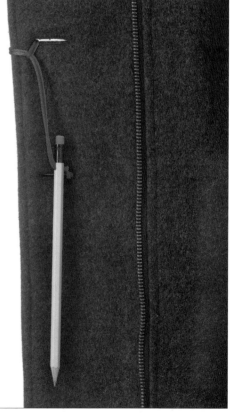

5 Gently pull the pencil through to complete the set-up.

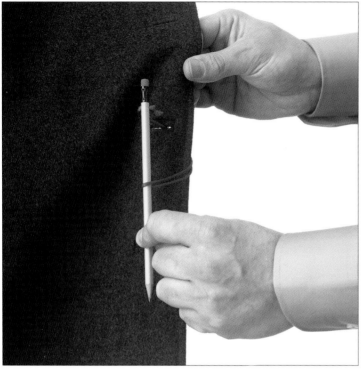

6 When your victim demands that you remove the pencil after failing miserably, do the following. Lift the pencil through the loop as far as it will go.

7 Pull the pencil out so that it is at right angles to the buttonhole, then push the top back through the buttonhole.

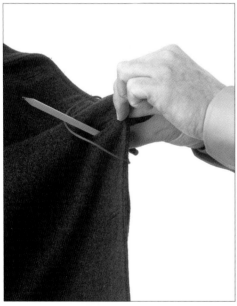

8 Hold on to the pencil and once again pull as much fabric as you can through the loop of string.

9 You will now be able to remove the pencil completely.

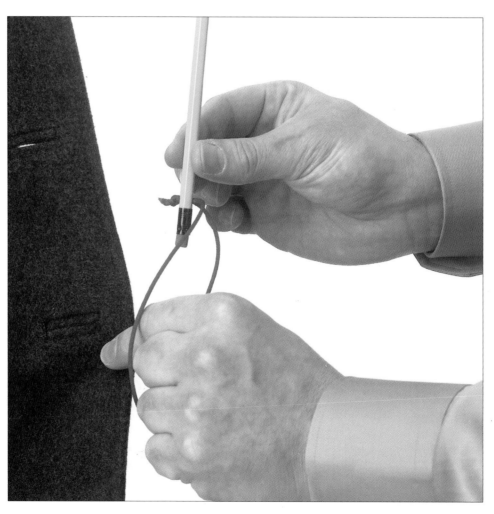

stand-up magic

You will need to choose material that can be seen and understood from a distance when performing stand-up magic. This is because the audience is likely to be larger than one you would perform stunts or tricks to. So, as a rule, small props should be avoided, but as you will see from the material in this chapter, many of the props are ordinary, everyday objects that many people already own.

introduction

The kind of performance described by the all-encompassing term "stand-up magic" could also be described as "cabaret magic", "parlour magic" or even "stage magic". Performances of this type may take place on a stage, a dance floor, in a hall, perhaps even in someone's living room, but the defining characteristic of all tricks in this genre is that they are suitable for a large audience. Often these performances make use of large props and sometimes members of the audience may be required to assist with the tricks.

Some of the tricks described in this chapter may well be suitable for close-up performances as well, but generally tricks are included in the stand-up magic category because they look better from a distance and, occasionally, distance is actually required to hide the method. Square Circle Production, for example, requires a small distance between the prop and the audience if the illusion is to be convincing.

As you begin to put an act together you may find that one or two of the items in the Illusions chapter can be included to complement your choice of tricks from this chapter. In fact sometimes there is a fine line between what constitutes a piece of stand-up magic and what should be defined as an illusion. The key to choosing material for your stand-up magic act is *visibility*. What you are doing must be highly visible to everyone watching.

However, your choice of material will also depend on the style of performance you choose to adopt. Will you be creating a comedy act? If so, you will want to make sure there are lots of visual effects throughout the show that can be presented in an amusing way. Items such Paper Balls over the Head, Candy Caper and Crazy Spots would all be perfect for this kind of act.

If you're going to try to convince your audience that you are a mind reader, your choice of material will definitely need careful planning. Incredible Prediction, Picture Perfect and Multiplication Sensation could be ideal for this scenario. Perhaps you have decided that your act will be silent and that you will perform to music. If so, Square Circle Production, Blended Silks and Vanishing Glass of Liquid could be seamlessly linked together to make a nice little routine.

If you have the benefit of an assistant, other options are available to you. The Incredible Blindfold Act, for example, could be incorporated with one of the illusions in the next chapter, to create a smoothly flowing and varied routine.

It is almost impossible to pinpoint the beginning of stand-up magic, since the very term means different things to different people. To some extent, changing performing environments have dictated the prevailing style of magic. Nowadays the world's leading magicians have theatres in which to perform, but before variety became fashionable in the theatre magic was often performed on the streets.

An early street magician who was perhaps one of the first successful stand-up performers in recorded history was Isaac Fawkes (1675–1731). He was a frequent attraction at outdoor fairs (including the famous Bartholomew Fair in London), where his performances would have enthralled the masses. It was perhaps at this time, as a result of Fawkes' success, that stand-up magic began to catch on and gather pace.

By the late 18th century it was not uncommon for audiences to enjoy a magic act at a theatre. The Italian magician Giuseppe Pinetti (1750–1800) was one of the first to perform in such a venue when he appeared in London. In the vaudeville era, which

MR. DEVANT.

Above: England's David Devant, the first president of The Magic Circle and regular performer at The Egyptian Hall in Piccadilly, London.

began in the mid-1800s, a large number of regular acts toured the world with their stand-up magic performances, stunning and delighting audiences everywhere. The late 19th and early 20th centuries were exciting times for conjuring and the period is known today as the Golden Era of Magic.

Dozens of renowned stand-up performers have featured in magic's rich history. Among the best were Chung Ling Soo (1861–1918), T. Nelson Downs (1867–1938), David Devant (1868–1941) and Okito (1875–1963). In more recent times the names of Cardini (1895–1973), Roy Benson (1914–77) and Fred Kaps (1926–80) are just a few of those whose manipulation and magical artistry ensure that they will always be remembered.

Among today's stars of stand-up magic there are several names that represent the peak of this type of work. Britain's Paul Daniels is one of these, and he has enjoyed more than ten successful years on television. Geoffrey Durham became famous during the 1980s in the guise of his comedy character the Great Soprendo, but he is now a star in his own right and a familiar face on television and in theatres across the UK.

Above: Stand-up magician Mac King combines family-friendly comedy with sleight-of-hand and visual gags to create a show that keeps everyone entertained. He performs regularly in Las Vegas, and has also appeared on several television shows.

Left: Derren Brown regularly appears on British television. This charming and stylish performer has the apparent ability to read people's minds and control their responses, and his remarkable abilities have made him a household name in the UK.

Wayne Dobson is another of Britain's finest magicians. Although he is now confined to a wheelchair after developing multiple sclerosis, he continues to perform and receives standing ovations from audiences all over the world.

One of my favourite stand-up magicians from the USA is Mac King. He performs his show daily at Harrah's Casino in Las Vegas. His act is clever, funny and amazing. Other superb stand-up magicians include the USA's Michel Finney, Mike Caveney and Jon Stetson, Britain's premier psychological illusionist Derren Brown and the comedy magician John Archer. In truth there are dozens of world-class stand-up magicians around now and maybe after working on some of the items in this chapter you will aspire to join them. Good luck!

production tube

A roll of card, which is opened and shown to be empty, is rolled back into a tube and used to produce silk handkerchiefs from thin air.

You can use this simple prop to make anything that fits inside the tube appear or disappear.

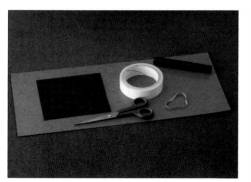

1 To make the tube you will need a piece of red card (stock) approximately 30 x 60cm (12 x 24in), a piece of black card approximately 10 x 15cm (4 x 6in), some double-sided adhesive tape, a pair of scissors, a rubber band and a pen.

2 Fold the red card in half across its width, making a sharp crease.

3 Attach a length of double-sided tape to one of the shorter sides of the black card. Starting from the opposite side, roll the card into a tube and secure it neatly with the tape.

4 With the red card still folded in half, roll it up tightly from the folded edge.

5 Secure the tube with a rubber band and leave overnight, so that when the band is removed the tube holds its shape.

6 Use a piece of double-sided tape to secure the black tube to the centre of the red card alongside the crease, as shown. This is a secret compartment that will never be seen by the spectators.

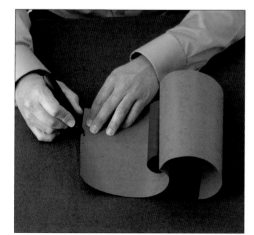

7 Mark a black dot on the red card, on the edge of the section with the secret compartment. Ensure the tube is oriented as shown here before you mark it.

8 Place the rubber band around the tube to hold it in place as you insert three coloured silks, one at a time, into the secret compartment.

9 Twist the ends of the silks together as they go into the tube. This will make it easier to remove them during the performance.

10 Once you have put all three silks inside the secret compartment remove the band and you are ready to perform the trick.

11 Begin by showing the tube of red card to the audience.

12 Pull the tube open, making sure that your right hand holds the edge with the black spot you made earlier.

secret view

13 The view from above shows exactly what is happening.

14 When the tube is fully unrolled it will look like a plain piece of card.

secret view

15 The secret compartment is hidden on the back.

16 Roll the card back up into a loose tube again.

17 Reach in and remove the first of the silk handkerchiefs.

18 Then remove the other silks and once again open the tube to show the audience that it is empty.

blended silks (version 1)

Four separate silks are pushed into an empty card tube. They come out joined together as one blended square. This is another trick you can do using the production tube with the secret compartment that is described on page 174.

1 Using double-sided adhesive tape, carefully join the edges of four silks to make a large square. Insert this special silk into the secret compartment of your production tube.

2 When you perform the trick, have four separate silks in the same four colours displayed in a wine glass and show the tube empty as described previously.

3 Pick up the separate silks one at a time, and insert them into the secret compartment on top of the prepared silk.

4 Slowly pull out the blended silk from the bottom of the tube.

5 Open it out to show that the four different-coloured silks have joined together as one.

6 Finish by opening the tube to show it empty. The separate silks are safely hidden in the secret compartment.

magic photo album

A photograph album is seen to be completely empty, only to be shown filled with pictures a few seconds later. This clever trick utilizes a principle called "short and long", which can be put to all sorts of uses in stand-up magic and card tricks.

1 Slice the edge off every other page in a photograph album. The first page should be cut short, the next left long, the next cut short, and so on.

2 Insert photographs into every other pair of pages, starting with pages 2 and 3, then 6 and 7, and so on.

3 Hold up the prepared album and explain to the spectators that you have some holiday snaps you would like to share with them.

4 If you open the album and flick through the pages from the back to the front, every page will appear blank. This is because you made every other page short and therefore the pages fall in pairs. The photographs are all located on the pages that are not seen.

5 Explain that the album is empty but you will use your magic to fill it up. Make a magical gesture and then open the album once again, but this time flick through the pages from the front to the back. Once again the pages will fall in pairs but now the blank pages will remain hidden and the album will appear to be full of pictures.

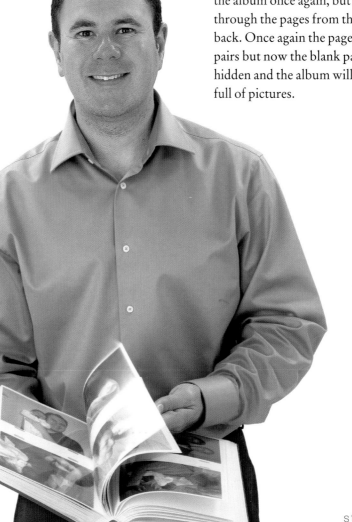

genie in a bottle

A bottle and a pencil are handed out for examination. The pencil is then dropped into the neck of the bottle and the genie is summoned. The genie, apparently with supernatural strength, holds on to the other end of the pencil so that the bottle remains suspended as it swings like a pendulum in the air. On the magician's command the

genie releases the pencil and once again everything is handed out for examination. Not surprisingly, no genie is found. A semi-transparent bottle has been used here so that you can see how the trick works, but you should use an opaque bottle to ensure that no one can see how it is accomplished.

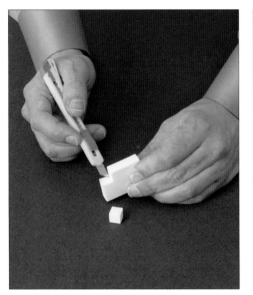

1 To prepare, begin by cutting a small cube from an eraser.

2 Sculpt this into a ball using a craft knife. The ball must fit comfortably inside the neck of the bottle you are going to use.

3 In performance, hand out the bottle and a pencil for examination. Meanwhile, secretly hold the ball loosely in the fingers of your right hand. This is called a "finger palm". Your hand must be held naturally and should not arouse any suspicion.

secret view

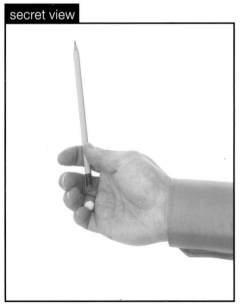

4 This view shows how the ball is hidden in your hand. There is no way it will be visible to the audience.

secret view

5 Take back the bottle with your left hand and insert the pencil into the bottle, allowing the rubber ball to fall inside at the same time. The reason the ball is made of rubber is so that it does not make a noise as it falls into the bottle.

6 Use you acting skills and say some magic words to summon the genie in the bottle.

7 Turn the bottle over: the ball will fall into the neck of the bottle and the pencil will trap it there.

8 Holding the pencil, let go of the bottle to show that the pencil is held inside, and swing the bottle from side to side.

9 To release the pencil simply push it down slightly and the ball will drop back into the bottle. Immediately remove the pencil.

10 As you offer the props for examination, turn the bottle upside down and allow the ball to fall out into the fingers of your left hand.

11 This secret view shows how the ball is held when it comes out of the bottle.

needles through balloon

A cardboard tube is shown empty. A long modelling balloon is inflated inside the tube so that both ends can be seen. Several long needles or skewers are pushed through the centre of the tube at all angles but the balloon does not burst. The needles are removed and the balloon is popped to finish the routine. There is more than one way of performing this trick; two of them are explained below.

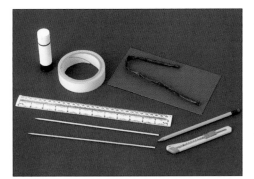

1 You will need a modelling balloon, a piece of card (stock), a ruler, a pencil, a knife, adhesive tape, skewers and some adhesive glue.

2 Mark out the card into five equal sections using a ruler so that you can create a square-section tube. (The size of this tube will depend on the size of the balloon you are using.)

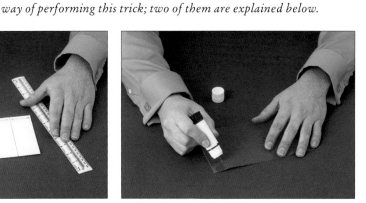

3 Apply glue to the inside of the last section and glue it over the first section to create the tube.

4 The finished card tube should look like this, and should be secure.

5 Using a craft knife, carefully make several star-shaped cuts in the card at different locations. Look at steps 10 and 11 to see the exact locations.

6 You can decorate your tube with a piece of coloured tape, if you wish.

7 In performance, show the balloon and the tube.

8 Blow up the balloon through the tube and knot the end. The balloon should be a snug fit in the tube but not too tight.

secret view

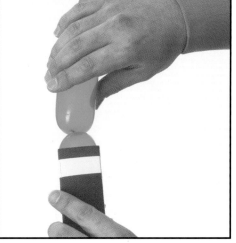

9 Secretly twist the balloon so that the twist is hidden inside the tube.

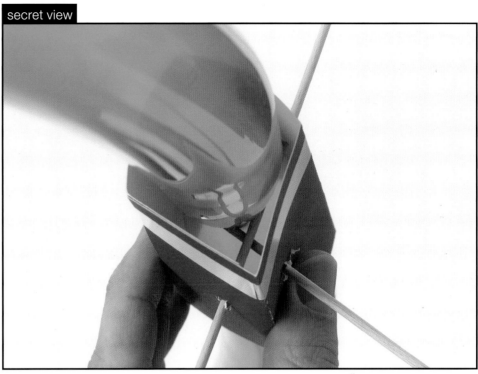

10 You can now push a skewer through one of the star-shaped cuts in the tube and out the other side. The twist in the balloon provides the space needed by the skewer.

11 Push another skewer in at a different angle. It looks as though it is impossible to do this without bursting the balloon. This secret view shows how the skewers go around the balloon inside the tube.

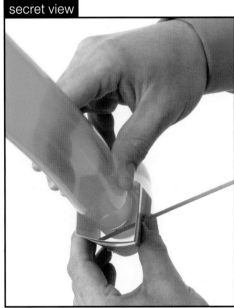

12 Modelling balloons are naturally flexible, so instead of twisting the balloon inside the tube (step 10) you can simply use the skewers to push it out of the way as they pass through the tube. This secret view shows how the skewer avoids the balloon as it enters. Notice how the balloon is pushed to one side.

13 The effect is identical. You can use either method – both work perfectly.

vanishing glass of liquid

A glass is filled with liquid from a jug (pitcher). The glass is covered with a handkerchief and tossed in the air, and both the glass and the liquid vanish instantly. This stunning trick requires two gimmicks to be made. The first is a special cloth, made from two identical layers

stitched or glued together, with a disc of cardboard in the middle. When held from above the illusion of a glass under the cloth is perfect. The second gimmick is a specially prepared jug, which only takes a few minutes to modify.

1 Draw around the glass you will be using on a piece of thick cardboard and cut out this circle.

2 Stick the cardboard disc to the centre of a small square of cloth. Then stick an identical cloth on top, sandwiching the disc in the middle.

3 The jug must be opaque, and should be big enough to hide the glass inside it. Line the inside of the jug with a bubble wrap bag. Leave the section nearest the spout unstuck.

secret view

4 This is how the prepared jug looks when you have lined it.

5 To prepare, pour some liquid into the jug between the unstuck portion of bubble wrap and the side of the jug.

6 Have the cloth folded, next to the prepared jug and the glass.

7 Pour the liquid into the glass, ensuring that the inside of the jug remains hidden from view.

8 Put the jug down just to the left of the glass. Pick up the prepared cloth, open it and turn it to show both sides.

9 Lay the cloth over the glass so that the cardboard disc (known to magicians as a "form") lies perfectly on top of the glass.

10 Lift the glass from above with your right hand and move it to your left. Note how the cloth passes directly over the jug. As it does, secretly drop the glass inside the jug and carry on moving to your left. The form will hold the shape of the glass beneath the cloth. Hold it between the right fingers and thumb.

11 You should now be moving away from the table and to the front of the stage. Count to three and toss the cloth into the air. The "vanish" is startling.

12 Catch the cloth and show it on both sides before putting it away and continuing with your programme.

going into liquidation

A glass of liquid vanishes, reappearing inside a box that was previously shown to be empty. This trick was originally performed *using a spectator's hat, but the box makes a good substitute. This trick uses the same gimmicked cloth as the Vanishing Glass of Liquid.*

1 Set the folded, gimmicked cloth inside a small box and have a glass of liquid to hand.

2 Show the glass of liquid to the spectators then cover it with your special cloth.

3 Pick up the box and show that it is empty.

tip *Because of the similarity of this trick with the Vanishing Glass of Liquid you will not want to have both in the same programme. However, when you are learning it is interesting to see how the same effect can be achieved using a variety of methods. Knowing more than one way to make something happen allows you to choose the best method for any given show.*

4 Say that the glass is going to fly to the box. As you say this, mimic the flight of the glass, holding it from above, and place the covered glass inside the box.

5 Leave the glass inside, removing only the cloth, which will maintain the shape of the glass. Move away and prepare to throw the glass up into the air.

6 Throw the cloth high above you, vanishing the glass of liquid.

7 Catch the cloth and show both sides to the audience.

8 Finally, reveal to your audience that the glass of liquid really is in the box as you promised it would be.

liquidated assets

Liquid is poured into an empty cardboard box, which magically remains totally dry. Like Going into Liquidation, this routine *originally used a borrowed hat. It is very effective, and uses cheap and easy-to-make props.*

1 Construct a simple gimmick by cutting the rim off a plastic cup.

2 Now cut the base out of a second plastic cup.

3 When these two cups are nested together they look like one.

4 Have your special cup and a jug (pitcher) of liquid on one table and the box on the other. Hold the cup and show the box empty and dry.

5 Explain to the spectators that there is an old trick during which the magician pours water into a cardboard box without damaging it. The secret, you go on to explain, is to sneak an empty cup into the box when no one is looking. Show the cup empty and put it into the box.

secret view

6 Now explain that you are going to do the trick without the cup! Reach into the box and remove the bottomless cup only (the inner cup). Make sure you do not "flash" the bottom of the cup to the spectators.

7 Pour some liquid from the jug, apparently into the box, but actually into the hidden cup. Suitable expressions help to sell the idea that the liquid is sloshing around the bottom of the box.

secret view

8 Take the cup and say you'll perform some magic. Put the cup into the box and in doing so, nest it inside the other one, which is now full of liquid.

9 Take the filled cup from the box and pour the liquid back into the jug with a flourish.

10 Finish by showing that the box is both empty and completely dry.

multiplication sensation

The last six digits of the number on a credit card are read out loud and multiplied by a number chosen by a spectator. The magician *shows a prediction, which was made before the show started. It matches the total exactly.*

1 You will need a slip of paper, a marker pen, a calculator, a pair of scissors and some adhesive tape.

2 Write the number 142857 on the paper, ensuring that you leave a small space between each digit.

3 Now carefully tape the edges of the paper together so that the digits are on the outside of the hoop. Use a pair of scissors to cut the tape neatly and apply it to the back of the paper only, so that the join is imperceptible.

4 In performance, display your prediction at your fingertips. No one should be able to see that the paper is one continuous loop of numbers. Place the prediction to one side or in a pocket.

5 Now take a credit card from your wallet and explain that you will read out the last six digits of the number. Pretend to read from the card, but instead call out the number 142857. Ask a spectator to enter this number into a calculator.

6 Ask your helper with the calculator to multiply the number by any whole number from 1 to 6. The secret is that no matter which number they multiply by, the answer will consist of the same six digits but in a different, cyclical order. It will be 285714, 428571, 571428, 714285 or 857142.

secret view

7 Once the answer is read out loud, secretly and quickly tear the paper between the appropriate numbers.

8 Display your prediction, which will match the total on the calculator.

spiked thumb

You cover your thumb with a paper napkin and display three long spikes. You proceed to skewer your thumb with these spikes and

finally show your thumb to be perfectly healthy. This is a simple trick that will elicit a huge response from your audience.

1 All you need for this gory and wonderful trick is a potato, some skewers, a paper napkin and a knife.

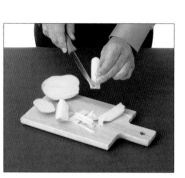

2 Use the knife to cut a chunk of potato into the approximate size and shape of your thumb.

secret view

3 To begin the trick, show the napkin in your right hand, with the potato hidden behind it.

4 From the front the potato cannot be seen. Hold up your left thumb in a "thumbs up" position.

secret view

5 Slide the napkin over your left hand and as you do so grab the potato in your fist so that it sticks up in place of your thumb.

6 Seen from the front it looks just as if you have your thumb stuck up under the napkin. The illusion is perfect.

7 Show the first skewer and prepare to push it into your "thumb".

8 Act as though you are in pain as the skewer goes right through.

9 Repeat this action several more times.

10 Finally remove the spikes, and prepare to whip off the napkin.

11 As you do so, pull the potato away unseen and at the same time stick up your undamaged thumb to complete the illusion.

tip *If you wanted to be really gross you could wrap a sachet of tomato sauce around the potato before beginning the trick to give an added touch of realism.*

square circle production

For this trick you need to make a clever prop that has endless uses. It is an ideal way to make something appear – anything that will fit inside the box. It has been used by magicians for generations and is incredibly deceptive. Its great advantage is that, unlike many other production boxes, you can use this one when surrounded by spectators. The illusion is so versatile that you can even make a giant one from which you can produce a person. You can also buy professional square circle production boxes from many magic shops.

1 You will need several sheets of cardboard in different colours, adhesive tape or glue, a pair of scissors or a knife and some black paint. First make a tube from a sheet of black cardboard.

2 Now make a larger tube from a sheet of blue cardboard: it needs to slip easily over the black tube and to be about 2.5cm (1in) taller.

3 You now need to construct a square tube that is the same height as the black tube and that will fit easily around the blue tube. Cut some slots out of the front panel of the box so the spectators will be able to see inside it.

4 This square tube should be painted black inside.

5 These are the separate pieces you should have: a square tube painted black inside, a blue tube that fits inside it, and a black tube that fits inside the blue one and is a little shorter.

6 Set up the trick by placing the blue tube over the black tube and the red tube over everything. Place the box on a table. The surface should be black, so you will need a black tablecloth or a mat large enough to set your Square Circle Production on. Put whatever you wish to produce by magic inside the black tube.

7 To begin, pick up the red tube and move it around to show the spectators that it is empty. Replace it in position around the blue tube.

8 Now pick up the blue tube and once again show that it is empty by pushing your arm through it. While you are doing this you can see that the black inner tube is invisible, as it looks like the inside of the red tube. This principle is called "black art" and is used in numerous magic tricks. When it is used properly no one should ever know there is anything there.

9 Replace the blue tube between the red one and the black one, say the magic words and then lift all three tubes together to reveal the item.

mini flip-flap production box

This small box can be shown empty and then used to produce anything that will fit inside it. In the next chapter you will see how

a larger version of the box can be used to make a person appear. If you are good at craft projects, you could make this box out of wood.

1 You will need some double-walled corrugated cardboard to make the box. Cut a rectangular panel as shown, approximately 15 x 30cm (6 x 12in) and fold it in the middle. Cut the centre out of one side: this will be the top of the box.

2 Now cut a second, identically sized panel and fold as before.

3 Tape the two panels together to make a box that will hinge flat.

4 Cut two 15cm (6in) square doors that fit the open sides of the box perfectly.

5 Make a second, smaller box approximately 5 x 5 x 7.5cm (2 x 2 x 3in) and glue it to one of the doors.

6 Attach the doors to the front and back of the box using adhesive tape, so that they flip open in opposite directions. The small box should be inside the main box when the door is closed.

7 Load the small box with the items you are going to produce. In this case it is silk handkerchiefs, and the ends are twisted together in order to make them easier to remove during the trick.

secret view

8 To begin the performance hold the box up with the loaded section on the back of the front door.

9 Open the box by moving your left hand to the left while your right hand stays where it is. This ensures that the loaded box is always shielded from view behind the door.

10 This is the view from the front. It looks as if you are showing a completely empty box. ▶

11 From the back the box now looks like this.

12 Continue to move the box all the way around, always keeping your right hand still so the box pivots around the loaded door.

13 Grip all the sections with your right hand to flatten the box, proving that it is empty.

14 From the front it looks as if it would be impossible to hide anything inside the box.

15 Reverse the moves to reassemble the box. Now make a magical gesture.

16 Reach into the hole in the top of the box and start to produce the silk handkerchiefs one at a time.

17 Of course you can use any object that will fit into the inner box.

18 If you wish, you can replace the silks in the box to finish the trick.

19 Open the doors to show the silks have vanished again. So this is not just a production box but a vanishing box too.

20 Don't forget to flatten the box, as this will make the vanishing effect even more convincing.

silk through glass (version 1)

A silk handkerchief penetrates the bottom of a glass. This is one of a variety of methods for performing this trick, and it is very effective.

Try practising in front of a mirror so that you make appropriate facial gestures, and work on your patter before you perform.

1 You should use the thinnest, most invisible thread you can find for this. Fishing line works very well. Prepare a silk handkerchief by attaching a short length of thread to one corner. This thread should be knotted at the end.

2 Display the silk in one hand (with the thread hidden in your hand) and a glass in the other.

3 Insert the handkerchief into the glass, allowing the thread to secretly trail out of the glass. ▶

4 This secret view shows how the thread should be positioned.

5 Show a second silk handkerchief in the other hand.

6 Place this on top of the first silk in the glass. Pick up a larger handkerchief.

7 Place the large handkerchief over the whole glass. Secure it with a rubber band around the mouth of the glass.

8 Lift up the large handkerchief to show the silks inside the glass.

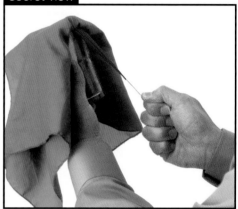

9 Reach underneath and feel for the trailing thread. Begin to pull down on the thread.

10 The bottom silk will be pulled out of the sealed glass, under the band and down towards your hand. Grip the corner of the silk and continue to pull it down. It will appear to be penetrating the bottom of the glass.

11 Lift the handkerchief to show the other silk still in position in the top of the glass.

12 Finally, remove the large handkerchief and the rubber band.

silk through glass (version 2)

This is a variation of the method used for the previous trick. This version uses no gimmicks at all. It can be performed totally *impromptu, as you should be able to find a glass and a few handkerchiefs or napkins in most places.*

1 Display a silk handkerchief in one hand and a glass in the other.

2 Insert the silk into the glass and prepare to cover everything with a larger, opaque handkerchief.

secret view

3 As soon as the glass is hidden out of sight, secretly allow it to swivel upside down.

4 Wrap a band around the base of the glass. (Your audience will assume it is the top of the glass.)

5 It is now easy to pull the silk down, creating the illusion that it is penetrating the base of the glass.

6 Pull the band and the handkerchief off the glass.

secret view

7 At the same time turn the glass back to the upright position while it is still concealed by the handkerchief.

8 You can finish by handing out everything for examination, if you wish.

switching bag

This clever bag can be used to switch objects, make things appear and even make them disappear. The bag is extremely simple to make, and if you wish to make a more professional looking, longer lasting bag, you could stitch rather than glue the material together.

1 Make the bag from felt. Start by cutting out a rectangle approximately 25 x 30cm (10 x 12in) and a smaller piece just a little less than 25cm (10in) square. Apply glue to the areas shaded in black.

2 Fold the rectangle in half, with the smaller square sandwiched in between. Ensure the pieces are securely glued so the bag won't fall apart during tricks.

3 You now have a bag with two sections. The central piece of fabric should be a fraction shorter than the two sides so that it cannot be seen.

4 To hide the central section turn the top 2.5cm (1in) of fabric inside out to create a "cuff" around the edge. This completes the bag.

picture perfect

In this trick the switching bag is used for a very simple yet effective mind-reading stunt in which you appear to be able to predict what someone will draw before they have drawn it. You could draw any common object, such as a flower or a smiley face.

1 Prepare by cutting approximately 24 small slips of paper. Half should be left blank and the other half should each have a house drawn on them. Make a larger picture of this house and seal it inside a prediction envelope.

2 Rest the envelope against a wine glass containing the blank slips of paper. Fold all the pre-drawn slips and place them inside one compartment of your switching bag. Fold back the top edges to form a "cuff", as previously described.

3 Show your prediction envelope and the slips of paper in the glass. Set the envelope down on the table and distribute the 12 blank slips, along with some pencils. Ask everyone to draw something simple on their slip of paper and then fold the paper in half.

4 Collect the slips of paper in the empty side of the bag, making sure that they can only put them in the empty side and that they can't see the secret compartment.

5 Bring the sides of the bag together and then shake to mix up the papers.

secret view

6 Stop shaking the bag and open the bag. As you do so, unfold the cuff and switch sides so that the slips of paper that you wrote on are accessible and the other predictions in the secret compartment are completely concealed.

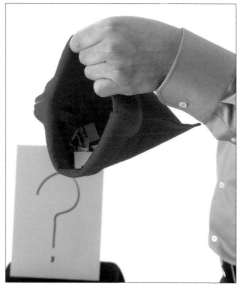

7 Fold the edges over the opposite way to hide the extra layer in the bag. Now ask someone to reach in and choose one of the slips. It will of course be one that you drew earlier.

8 Ask them to open the slip and tell everyone what it is. When they say, "A house," open your prediction envelope and show that you have drawn a house too. (Someone is likely to draw a house as there are only a few things people will draw off the cuff. Even if no one draws a house they will assume someone else did!)

blended silks (version 2)

Four separate silks are placed in the empty bag. They come out joined together as one blended square. Some magic shops stock "Blendo" *silks, which are made up of a mixture of colours specifically for tricks like this one, and are a good investment.*

1 Using double-sided tape carefully join together four silks, in four different colours, along the edges to make one large square.

2 Put this blended silk into one side of your switching bag.

3 Turn over the cuff so that the empty side is open.

4 Display four separate silks, matching the four in the blended square, in a wine glass.

5 Turn the bag inside out to show the audience that it is empty.

6 Now place the separate silks in the bag's empty compartment one at a time.

7 When the silks are all inside the bag make a magical gesture.

secret view

8 At the same time as you open the bag, switch compartments.

9 Reach into the secret compartment to pull out the blended silk.

10 Hold up the silk by the edges and wait for the applause!

candy caper

This is my favourite use for the switching bag. A glass of confetti is poured into the bag. A magic word is said and the confetti changes *into colourful candy that you can share with your audience. This trick is perfect for a children's show.*

1 Prepare the switching bag by filling the secret compartment with small candies. Fill a glass with paper confetti and have it on your table. Show the audience that your bag is empty.

2 Let the colourful confetti fall from a height into the empty side of your bag.

3 Give the bag a shake and simultaneously switch the sides.

4 Pour out the candy from a modest height, so that everyone can hear it hitting the sides of the glass.

5 There's only one thing left to do: offer the candy to your audience and help them eat it.

escapologist

Despite your hands being tied together with a handkerchief, you are able to escape from a rope that secures you. This is a great trick but *you must practise it a lot if you are to make it deceptive. The method is similar to the one used in Interlocked.*

1 Ask a spectator to tie your wrists together with a handkerchief or silk.

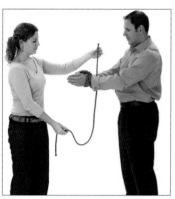

2 Now ask them to thread a length of rope between your arms.

3 They hold on to the ends and pull to confirm that you cannot escape.

secret view

4 Just before they pull, you must work a little piece of the rope between the heels of your palms, as shown.

5 Move your hands to the left and right to show you can't escape but as you move, work the rope further into your hands.

secret view

6 This is clearly shown in this close-up view.

7 The movement of your arms hides the fact that you are now slipping the rope over your left hand.

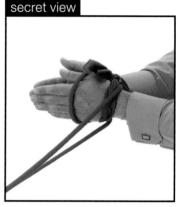

secret view

8 Again, this close-up shows exactly what is happening.

secret view

9 Once the rope is over your hand, pull back sharply: the rope will work its way under the handkerchief on the side of your hand.

10 You will be released from the rope, but you can show that your wrists are still genuinely tied together.

lord of the rings

A solid ring links on to a length of rope whose ends are firmly tied to your wrists. Here, the ring was made of rope but you could use a *bangle or any other object that fits over your wrist. Avoid performing both this trick and Escapologist in the same show.*

1 You will need two identical rings and a length of rope.

secret view

2 Prepare by placing one of the rings over your wrist and hiding it up your right sleeve.

3 In performance have someone tie one end of the rope around each of your wrists. Show the ring and explain that you will get it on to the rope. Of course, this sounds impossible.

4 Ask someone to cover your hands with a large cloth.

secret view

5 Under cover of the cloth (removed here for clarity) secretly hide the loose ring inside your shirt.

secret view

6 Pull the duplicate ring out of your sleeve, over your wrist and on to the length of rope.

7 Remove the cloth to show you have caused one solid object to penetrate another.

magic circles

One of the most famous magic tricks of all time is Chinese Linking Rings. In this simplified version, hoops of cloth magically double in size and join together. Use plain woven cotton that will tear easily *along the weave – a strip from an old bed sheet would be ideal. This is very cost effective as you will be able to make up several sets of hoops from just one sheet.*

1 You will need a strip of cotton 10cm (4in) wide and 1.5m (5ft) long. Prepare it by making a cut approximately 10cm (4in) deep in the middle of one end. Repeat this at the other end.

2 Apply strips of double-sided adhesive tape along the edge at one end.

3 Twist the right-hand side of the strip through 180 degrees (a half twist) before joining it neatly to the opposite end of the strip.

4 Twist the left-hand section through 360 degrees (a full twist) before joining it to the opposite end.

5 Finish the preparation by making 7.5cm (3in) slits through the centre of the divided sections on each side.

6 In performance show the hoop of cloth, hiding the prepared section in your hand.

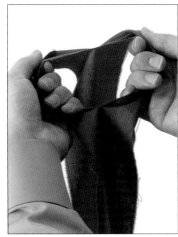

7 Tear the hoop exactly in two by pulling the two halves apart, starting at the divided section.

8 This is the view as seen from the front.

9 When you have torn the strips the result will be two separate hoops, one in each hand.

10 Place the fully twisted hoop over your shoulder and tear the half-twisted hoop into two again. Your tear should start from the slit you prepared earlier.

11 This will result in a giant hoop, twice the size of the original.

tip *If you prepare two cloth hoops, one regular and one with your special twists, you can invite a spectator to copy every move you make. While they keep halving the size of their hoops you can link and grow yours.*

12 Tear the remaining, fully twisted hoop in half.

13 Two hoops will form, one linked to the other.

crazy spots!

A normal, flat piece of card is shown to have four sides! This clever trick also has a great surprise ending. It is called a "sucker effect" as your audience thinks you are explaining how the trick works and then you surprise them with a twist at the end.

1 To prepare the trick you need to begin with three sheets of black card (stock), all identical in size: about 20 x 15cm (8 x 6in) is perfect.

2 Fold two of the pieces of card in half and glue them together as shown.

3 Glue this T-shaped piece on to the third sheet of card to create a flap that can be positioned up or down.

4 Cut out 15 circles from a sheet of white paper. These will be the domino spots.

5 Glue two spots on to one side of the flap, as shown.

6 Fold the flap over and glue eight spots on this section.

7 Place a tiny piece of double-sided tape at the top of this side. When you fold up this flap it will be held shut by the tape.

8 Turn the whole thing over and glue five spots on this side, as shown.

9 To perform the trick, start by holding the "domino" in your right hand so that your fingers cover the blank space. It will look as though you have six spots on view.

10 Bring your left hand up to the card from behind, to cover the blank space at the bottom of that side.

11 Turn the card with your left hand to show "three" spots on that side.

12 Grip the domino with your right hand so that your hand hides the centre spot on the reverse side.

13 Turn the card to show "four" spots.

14 Your left hand hides the bottom spot on the other side and once again turns the card.

15 This time only one spot can be seen.

16 Now you explain to your audience how the trick works by showing how three spots or one spot can be seen depending on where you place your hands.

secret view

17 Turn the card over and repeat the explanation for six spots or four. At the same time, secretly detach the tape from the flap and carefully flip the secret flap down.

18 All this should remain unseen by your audience, who are looking at the front of the card.

19 As you finish your explanation, turn the card over to reveal eight spots all over it!

trooping the colours

Although you try to sort small balls into their different colours, they seem to get jumbled up in the most bizarre fashion. This is quite a

long trick to remember, but lots of practice will ensure a smooth and baffling performance. Patter will help to keep spectators entranced.

1 You will need three coloured boxes and three small balls of each colour. Rolled-up tissue paper works perfectly. Set out the props as shown here.

2 Pick up the blue ball in the fingertips of your right hand and prepare to drop it inside the blue box.

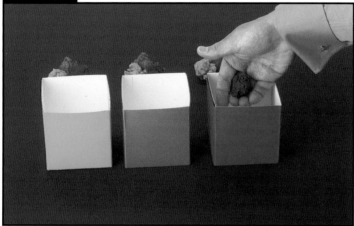

secret view

3 As your hand goes into the box and out of sight, secretly position the ball behind your fingers and remove your hand.

4 With the blue ball still secretly palmed, pick up the orange ball and prepare to place it in the orange box.

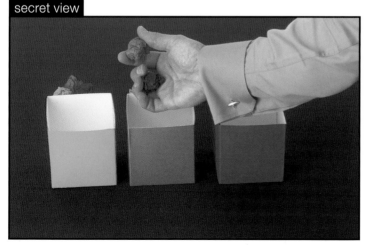

secret view

5 As your hand goes into the box switch balls and drop the blue ball inside.

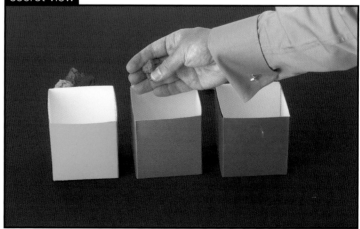

secret view

6 The orange ball now remains hidden in your hand as you lift your hand up.

7 Pick up the green ball and supposedly drop that inside the green box.

8 In fact you switch balls once again, and drop the orange ball, retaining the green one secretly in your hand.

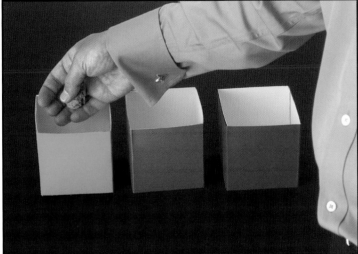

9 Remove your hand, secretly holding the green ball. Start the sequence again. First pick up the blue ball and put it in the blue box, switching it for the green ball, then pick up the orange ball and actually drop it in. Now pick up the green ball and switch it for the blue ball in your hand. The final time, you pick up the blue ball and actually place it in the blue box, pick up the orange ball and switch it for the green ball as it goes into the orange box, and finally pick up the green ball and actually put it in the green box.

10 The right hand still secretly holds an orange ball. Add this to the blue box as you tip the outer boxes upside down and let the contents fall out.

11 Finally tip the balls out of the centre box. The balls should all match their boxes but it seems the colours have mixed themselves up again.

paper balls over the head

Three paper balls vanish one at a time in the most impossible way. This trick was made famous by one of magic's greatest exponents, Tony Slydini. He was a master of misdirection and in his hands this one magic trick could entertain the biggest audiences. The trick can be done with

all sorts of objects, but it needs careful practice and rehearsal with a friend. It is a strange routine in that the only person fooled by the trick is the volunteer who is on stage with you. Your whole audience will see how this trick is done.

1 Invite a spectator on to the stage and sit them side-on to the audience. Give them a paper ball to hold in each hand and hold a third in the fingertips of your right hand.

2 Explain that you are going to put the paper ball into your left hand and that it will disappear on the count of three. Actually place the ball in your left hand as you speak. Take it back into your right hand and start the count.

3 Each time you count out loud, raise your right hand just above the volunteer's eyeline. On "Three", gently toss the ball over their head as your hand moves up.

4 Immediately pretend to place the ball in your left hand and close it as if it contains the ball. If you have succeeded, your volunteer will not have seen the ball tossed over their head and will believe it is in your left hand.

5 Open both hands to show they are empty.

6 Repeat the sequence with one of the balls the volunteer is holding.

7 And one final time. Each time it seems to be more impossible than the last time.

8 The volunteer will be amazed.

incredible prediction

Three coloured cards are shown and a spectator is asked to choose one. You prove that you knew beyond a doubt which colour they would opt for. It is based on the principle known among magicians as a "multiple out", as the trick can end in a number of different ways.

It has been applied to thousands of tricks and is extremely effective and supremely baffling. Of course you must never perform this trick again to the same audience as they will be aware of the various outcomes and will work out how the trick is done.

1 You will need an envelope and some sheets of coloured card (stock): two orange, two blue and one yellow. Prepare the envelope by sticking one orange card to the back.

2 Put a large "X" on the back of the yellow card.

3 Insert the two blue cards, one yellow card (with the "X" on the back) and one orange card into the envelope.

4 Draw a large question mark on the front of the envelope and explain to your audience that you are about to prove that you can accurately predict a future event.

5 Reach into the envelope and remove three cards (orange, blue and yellow), leaving the duplicate blue card secretly inside.

6 Keep the envelope in view, being careful not to flash the orange card on the back of it. Fan out the three colours and ask a spectator to choose which colour they want. Make sure you give them a chance to change their mind.

7 If they choose blue, ask someone to reach inside the envelope and remove the contents. It will be a blue card and you will have proved you knew what their choice would be. (Again, be careful not to flash the orange card on the back of the envelope.)

8 If orange is their choice, turn the envelope around to reveal your prediction on the back.

9 Finally, if yellow was chosen turn all the cards around and show the large "X" on the back of the yellow card, again proving you knew which one it would be.

vanishing mug of liquid

A mug filled with liquid is turned upside down on a spectator's head. The liquid disappears, leaving the mug empty. Be careful not to show the inside of the mug when you do this trick, and make sure your helper receives a round of applause for being such a great sport.

1 Cut out the absorbent section of a disposable nappy (diaper). This contains crystals that are able to absorb many times their own weight in liquid.

2 Add some double-sided adhesive tape to the underside of the nappy and stick it inside a mug with a white interior. The nappy will be a tight fit so you will need to pack it in.

3 Set the prepared mug and a jug (pitcher) of liquid on a table with a sheet of card. Invite a spectator to join you on stage and sit them down next to you.

4 Slowly pour about half a mugful of liquid into the mug. The nappy will absorb everything.

5 Explain to everyone that you are going to demonstrate a science experiment with some liquid and some card.

6 Lay the piece of card on top of the mug of liquid.

7 Turn everything upside down, using a quick but smooth action.

8 Place the mug and the card on your volunteer's head.

9 Slip out the card, but then admit that you've forgotten exactly how the experiment works!

10 However, as you're a magician it is easy to make the liquid disappear. Simply say some magic words and slowly lift the mug up into the air. The liquid will have vanished.

incredible blindfold act

This routine is really offered for laughs rather than as a serious mind-reading illusion. Even so, right until the end your audience will wonder how your assistant is able to tell which objects are being held up in the air while they are blindfolded. When you ask your assistant what you are holding, they should not just say, "You are holding a watch," but something like, "I am getting the sense of movement, a sweeping motion, yes, of something moving but very small movements. In fact I see time passing slowly. Yes, the movement I see is a hand on a watch. This is a watch." Building it up like this adds a believability factor to the magic trick, which only makes it funnier when the spectators see how it was done. The success of the trick depends on how good your assistant's acting skills are.*

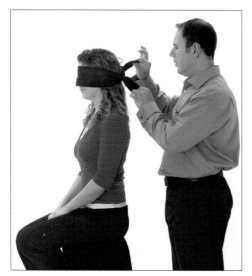

1 Your assistant is seated side-on to the audience and blindfolded with a thick black cloth.

2 Objects are borrowed from various members of the audience and held up in the air in front of the assistant. Despite being blindfolded, the assistant is able to explain which objects have been chosen.

3 When you stand and take a bow with your assistant at the end, everyone laughs as they see a big hole in the side of the blindfold that was hidden until this point.

watch this!

A watch disappears, only to reappear on your wrist moments later. The cloth used in this trick is know as a "Devil's handkerchief".

It can be used to make lots of things disappear in a very convincing fashion and is used by professional magicians.

1 Make a double cloth by stitching two identical cloths together around the edges, leaving half of one edge open.

2 Prepare for the trick by placing two identical watches on your wrist. One should be hidden up your sleeve and the other on view.

3 Position the cloth over your shoulder so that your fingers can immediately grasp the unstitched section.

4 When you start to perform the trick, remove the visible watch.

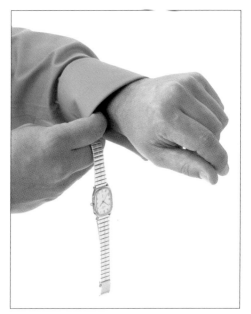

5 As you pull your sleeve down, secretly pull the other watch further down your arm to your wrist. No one will notice this.

6 Pull the cloth off your shoulder with your left hand, ensuring that you grip the open section. Hold the cloth open to display it. The watch is held between the fingers of your right hand.

7 Gather up the corners of the cloth to form a little bag.

8 Drop the watch into the secret pocket. It looks just as if it is dropping into the folds of the cloth.

9 Drop all the corners except for the one in your left hand (which is the prepared corner).

10 Show the cloth back and front. The watch is safely and totally hidden in between the two layers.

11 Finally, drape the cloth over your right arm and pull back your left sleeve to show the watch back on your wrist.

second sight

A shuffled deck of cards is placed in a brown paper bag and held high above the magician's head. Despite the apparent fairness of the shuffling procedure, the cards are named one at a time before being removed from the bag. This is a very deceptive trick and extremely baffling. You could also make an interesting presentation by pretending that you can see with your fingertips.

1 Cut a small square out of the bottom right corner of a brown paper bag.

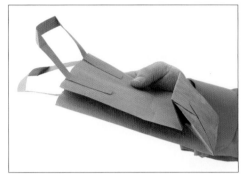

2 When the bag is folded flat the hole is hidden perfectly.

3 You can open the bag and show that it is empty. Just put your finger over the hole and keep the bag moving. No one will notice the tiny piece missing.

4 Have a deck of cards thoroughly shuffled and then clearly place them inside the paper bag.

5 Hold the bag up high over your head and explain that you will be using a technique called second sight to establish which card you are going to pull out.

secret view

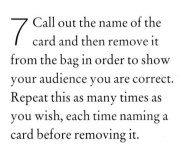

6 As you reach into the bag, glimpse the bottom card of the deck through the hole. This is the card you will remove.

7 Call out the name of the card and then remove it from the bag in order to show your audience you are correct. Repeat this as many times as you wish, each time naming a card before removing it.

Excalibur's cup

A plastic cup is placed on top of a book and a child is asked to lift it. They do, without a problem. You place a silk handkerchief in the cup and explain that you will hypnotize an adult into believing that the silk weighs a tonne and they will be unable to lift the cup. Unbelievably, they can't! You can enhance the presentation by creating a story that provides a reason or "plot" for the effect.

1 Cut a small hole, big enough for you to fit your thumb through, in the bottom of a plastic cup, as shown.

2 Set the cup on a book with the hole hidden at the rear and ask a child to lift up the cup. They do. Ask them to replace it.

secret view

3 Insert your thumb into the hole and secretly pin the cup to the book. Show a silk and place it inside the cup.

4 Now ask someone else to raise the cup off the book. They will be unable to do so.

anti-gravity glasses

Two ordinary glasses, which can be examined by the spectators, are placed on a book but don't fall off when it is turned upside down, *apparently defying gravity. This is a very old trick, which has baffled audiences for many years.*

1 You will need two plastic tumblers, two beads, some fine thread, a handkerchief, two silks, a pair of scissors and a hardback book.

2 To prepare the trick, tie the two beads together with thread, leaving a length of approximately 2.5cm (1in) between them. (This length may need adjusting to suit the size of your hand.)

3 Make a small slit in the hem of a handkerchief, or open a little of the stitching, and insert the two beads. Work them down to the middle of one of the edges.

4 To perform, show the tumblers to the spectators, then insert a silk into each one. Show the handkerchief, then lay it flat on the table. The beads should be at the edge opposite you. Place a hardback book horizontally in the centre of the handkerchief on the table.

5 Fold the left side of the handkerchief neatly over the edge of the book, as shown here.

6 Now fold the other side of the handkerchief over the edge of the book too.

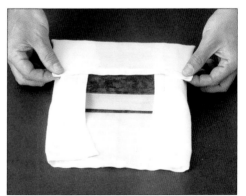

7 Bring the side of the handkerchief nearest you up over the edge of the book.

8 Finally the side with the beads should be folded over.

9 Pick up the book, gripping it and the handkerchief as shown. Place your thumb directly between the two beads.

10 Take one of the plastic tumblers with a silk inside.

11 Turn it upside down and position it on the book so that the rim goes over one of the beads and rests against your thumb. Notice how a small corner of silk is protruding from the tumbler. Repeat with the second tumbler.

12 Turn everything upside down, supporting the tumblers with your other hand, but then let go.

13 The tumblers are pinned in place between the beads and your thumbs, so they will remain suspended.

14 Slowly pull out one of the coloured silks to prove the tumblers are not connected to the book.

15 Repeat the action and remove the other silk.

16 Pause for a moment to add drama to the performance.

17 Turn the book over and remove the tumblers one at a time.

18 Unwrap the book. Everything apart from the handkerchief can be examined.

stage illusions

The term used to describe big, choreographed tricks is an "illusion". Cutting an assistant in half or making them appear to levitate are both good examples. Although this category of magic can be an expensive one to specialize in, it need not cost you much to make a few illusions for yourself. Here, you will discover the secrets of several basic tricks that look impressive when performed with confidence.

introduction

As a specialized area of magic, illusion pertains to the performance of magic tricks on the largest scale. Often involving at least one other person, in many cases several, and sometimes animals such as doves, tigers and even elephants, illusions usually require large props such as cabinets and boxes. They include sawing people into two or more pieces, defying gravity by suspending or levitating a person, animal or object, and causing objects or people to vanish into thin air or appear from nowhere. The scope of illusions is huge, and they have seen a resurgence in popularity in recent times, not least as a result of them being televised.

It is generally agreed among magicians that there are seven categories of illusion, namely, *production*, *vanish*, *transformation*, *restoration*, *teleportation*, *levitation* and *penetration*, although some magicians think that *penetration* is a separate category of magic, while others think it falls in the *teleportation* or *restoration* categories. All illusions, whatever their scale, are based on one or other of these seven basic elements. Some may incorporate more than one, but essentially every illusion you will ever see could be pigeon-holed into one of these categories.

Above: Although this magician is using minimal props to apparently levitate his assistant, this trick would still be reasonably expensive to perform.

Below: An old picture of a magician suspending his assistant from a broomstick at an impossible angle!

Above: A female magician impaled on a giant screw during a recorded performance for German television. This is a good example of how effective large scale stage illusions can be. The techniques used for this stunt are a closely guarded professional secret, and this should never be attempted at home.

Illusions can be expensive to stage. It is not unusual for an illusionist to require elaborate props that must be built to suit their unique specifications, and then, of course, there is the storage and transportation of these items to consider. The magician must also take into account the number of assistants that are needed to set up, perform and stage an entire illusion show, as well as any technicians that may be required to operate lighting or other stage effects.

The way in which this sphere of magic has developed and evolved since illusion shows first became popular during the 19th century is particularly interesting. Among the first illusionists to entertain audiences with their novel spectacles were Jean Eugène Robert-Houdin (1805–71), John Nevil Maskelyne (1839–1917), Buatier De Kolta (1847–1903), Harry Kellar (1849–1922), Charles

Right: French magician Jean Eugène Robert-Houdin was one of the most famous illusionists of the 19th century, and today he is known as 'the father of modern magic'. His habit of performing in theatres and private parties and wearing formal attire is still adopted by many magicians, and he is said to have so inspired a little-known young Hungarian magician, Erich Weiss, that he made his stage name Harry Houdini in tribute to him.

Morritt (1861–1936), Charles Carter (1874–1936), Howard Thurston (1869–1936), Harry Houdini (1874–1926), Dante (1883–1955) and many more.

The story of Harry Houdini's Metamorphosis stunt is a great example of the way in which illusions have evolved over a period of time. Before Houdini became best known as an escapologist, he performed this act with his brother, Theo. Harry would be handcuffed and would then step into a large cloth bag before being locked inside a huge chest or trunk. This was in turn bound with rope and padlocked. A large curtain would then be closed around the chest and Theo would step behind the curtain. Three seconds later the curtain would open to reveal Harry, having escaped from the chest. The rope was then untied, the box and bag unlocked and opened and out stepped Theo.

This great trick was invented by the British illusionist John Nevil Maskelyne, around 1860. Houdini gave it the name Metamorphosis and made it his own. Since then the illusion, also known as a substitution ("sub") trick, has featured in just about every illusionist's act at one time or another. It is definitely one of the most amazing illusions ever

created. Modern touches and twists are countless, as different performers experiment with the shape of the box, the method and the curtain, to name just a few of the changes that have been tried.

There is one act that performs Houdini's Metamorphosis faster than anyone else in the world to date. The Pendragons from the USA have taken the illusion so far forward that it would probably even stun Houdini if he were alive to see it. In the Pendragons' version, members of the audience are invited to check a box, before the magician is tied securely in a sack, then chained and locked inside the box. The assistant then steps up on top of the box and raises a curtain.

This is where the Pendragons' version of the trick surpasses all others. The curtain is thrown into the air for literally a fraction of a second before being ripped in two to reveal that the transformation has occurred and the assistant has disappeared. The box is then opened and the assistant steps out, having somehow found the time to change costumes as well.

The Pendragons remain one of the most successful and incredible illusion acts of our times. Other current major illusionists include the Americans David Copperfield and Lance Burton, Hans Klok

of the Netherlands, Portugal's Luis de Matos and Italy's Silvan. Las Vegas is considered to be the magic Mecca of the world. Most major illusionists have performed their show at one or other of the myriad hotels that line the strip.

The world-famous illusionists Siegfried and Roy performed at the Mirage in Las Vegas for 13 years until one of their white tigers attacked Roy during a performance on stage on 3 October 2003. This near-fatal incident led to the closure of their show after nearly 6,000 performances during an incredibly successful 30-year partnership.

While many illusions cost vast sums of money to create and perform, it doesn't have to cost a lot to build and make your own illusion. Among the pages that follow in this chapter you will find many simple, cheap illusions that require only a little searching for the right equipment and some time to make the props.

The New York magic dealer and inventor U. F. Grant published a booklet called *Victory Carton Illusions* in the mid-1900s, which contained many illusions that could be achieved using cardboard boxes. Some of the ideas in this chapter stem from that collection of illusions.

Above: Lance Burton is one of America's foremost magicians. Having performed in Las Vegas for nine years, he went on to win the F.I.S.M., and makes regular television appearances as well as performing daily in Las Vegas.

Above: Las Vegas legends Siegfried & Roy with one of their rare and frighteningly powerful white tigers before their accident in 2003. They are among the best-known illusionists in the world.

It is unlikely that you will want to make or perform every trick in this chapter, and nor should you feel you have to. Simply choose one or two illusions that will help to make your show more substantial and give it a professional look. You will probably find that some of these illusions are more suited to your requirements than others.

You should think about who you will be performing to when you select an illusion, and you could perhaps adapt the props accordingly. For instance, you could decorate the boxes used in several of the tricks.

Whatever your preference, I think you will enjoy reading and learning how to cut someone in half with ropes, how to make someone float, and how to make your assistant magically appear on stage with you.

Right: An old Thurston promotional poster from the early 1900s. Original magic posters are very desirable collectables and often sell for vast sums of money at auctions and on the internet. This one illustrates Thurston's latest show-stopping illusion – the floating lady.

Below: South African-born Robert Harbin performing Sawing a Lady in Half. Harbin created some of the most popular illusions used by magicians today, including the Zig-Zag Lady, in which a woman's middle is inexplicably pushed over to one side during the course of the performance.

comedy levitation

Your audience will gasp in amazement when they see you levitate your assistant – and laugh too if you show them how you did it. It is *generally bad practice to expose a magic trick for the sake of a laugh, but this is more of a gag than a serious illusion.*

1 To prepare the illusion, cut two full-size leg shapes out of an old cardboard box.

2 Put a pair of your assistant's shoes on the ends of the fake legs and get them to hold the legs out in front of them, parallel to the ground. They will also need to lean their head back as far as possible to look as if they are lying down.

3 Cover your assistant in a sheet from the neck down. The sheet must cover the point where their feet touch the floor. The illusion of levitation is uncanny. You can either float your assistant across the stage and off the other side, or "accidentally" step on the sheet so that when your assistant moves across the stage the cloth is pulled off to reveal the method.

tip *Your assistant can be prepared off-stage and float on to the stage at any point during your performance. If they bend their knees and bob up and down it will enhance the illusion of weightlessness.*

mini me

This is another funny routine to use as part of a larger act. The curtains open, and there on the stage is a miniature, dancing, moving mini version of your assistant or yourself, depending on who is standing in front.

1 Stand in front of a table and put your arms into a pair of trousers. The waistband should rest on your shoulders. Put your hands into a pair of shoes.

2 Now drape a jacket, back to front, around your shoulders.

3 Have your assistant who is kneeling behind you put their arms through the arms of the jacket. From the front they will remain unseen.

4 If the two of you coordinate your movements you can devise some really funny things for your Mini Me to do. Even simple things like running your hands through your hair look strange.

5 Try levitating off the table by simultaneously lifting the shoes up and fluttering your hands.

6 You can move from side to side and play with different objects. This is good fun to try out.

Houdini outdone!

Houdini was famous for escaping from locks, chains, prison cells and mailbags. In this version of one of his tricks, the escapologist is tied up inside a sack but manages to escape in double-quick time. This trick is incredibly simple to learn as well as being a real show stopper.

secret view

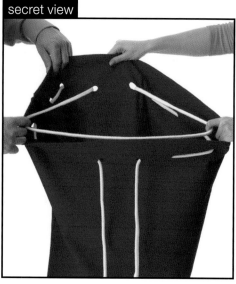
secret view

1 You will need a sack large enough for your escapologist to climb into. If necessary you can simply make your own from some cheap, porous opaque fabric. There should be a number of holes around the top of the sack through which you need to thread a rope.

2 Leave some slack in the rope, and hide this extra length inside the sack.

3 The extra loop should be equal to the circumference of the sack.

4 Prepare by arranging a screen on stage, and lay the sack out on the floor ready to step into.

5 The escapologist climbs into the sack and crouches down.

6 The assistant pulls the sack up over the escapologist's head.

7 This is what happens inside the sack: the escapologist steps on the extra loop of rope hidden inside.

8 The assistant pulls the rope ties the bag up. (The extra rope is still held under the escapologist's foot in the sack.)

9 Now the assistant places a screen in front of the sack and waits.

secret view

10 The escapologist releases the loop of rope and uses the slack to open the sack to escape.

secret view

11 After escaping, the escapologist reseals the sack by pulling on the rope.

secret view

12 The excess rope is then slipped back into the bag, leaving the knots at the front intact.

13 The escapologist walks in front of the screen holding the sack and receives the well-deserved applause.

flip-flap production

Illusions don't have to be expensive to build. Here is a way to make someone appear using nothing more than a large cardboard carton.

Now all you need to do is find a willing assistant and teach them how to perform this impressive trick.

1 Start with a tube of cardboard, simply made by cutting the top and bottom flaps off a large carton.

2 Tape a door to the front so that it swings freely in both directions.

3 Tape another door to the back, which should be hinged from the opposite side of the box.

4 Sit an assistant inside the box and close the doors. The illusion is ready.

5 Start the performance by opening the back door of the box.

secret view

6 As you can see from this secret view, your assistant is inside but unseen by your audience.

7 As you open the back door, the assistant crawls out of the box and behind the door, being very careful not to be seen.

8 When the front door is opened the box looks perfectly empty. Remember, your assistant is completely hidden behind the back door.

9 Crouch down at the back so everyone can see you through the box.

10 Close the front door of the box. Your assistant now crawls back inside the box.

11 Close the back door and make a magical gesture over the box.

12 Open the front door once again to reveal your assistant.

bowl vanish

Your assistant walks on to the stage carrying a big bowl on a tray. You show the audience a jug (pitcher) and pour its contents into the bowl. After covering the bowl with a large cloth you lift it off the tray and walk to the front of the stage. On a count of three you throw the cloth into the air with a flourish: the bowl of liquid vanishes completely! This clever illusion has been used by many of the world's

greatest magicians and although you need to prepare several gimmicks, they are easy to make and the illusion is not too difficult to perform. Its success depends on how well you make the props and how much you rehearse with your assistant. Teamwork is the key word here. Although your assistant doesn't seem to do much, in reality they do most of the work while you take all the credit.

1 Draw around the top of the bowl you are using, then cut out a disc of stout cardboard just a tiny bit larger – 3mm (⅛in) all round.

2 This "form" needs to be attached to the centre of a large square of cloth. You can do this using double-sided adhesive tape. Attach a second identical cloth, so that the cardboard form is sandwiched between the layers. You can stitch around the edges but it is easier and quicker to use iron-on fusible bonding web.

3 Fold the cloth neatly around the form so that it cannot be seen, and place the cloth to one side while you prepare the other props.

4 Cut out the absorbent section of a disposable nappy (diaper). This contains crystals that can absorb many times their own weight in water.

5 Use double-sided adhesive tape to secure the nappy inside the bowl. Push it well down below the rim so that it will not be seen.

6 Apply a big ball of reusable putty adhesive to the underside of the bowl.

7 Position the bowl in the centre of a tray, pressing it down firmly to make sure it is securely attached.

8 To complete the set-up, place a jug (pitcher) of liquid and the prepared cloth on the tray beside the bowl.

9 In performance, your assistant walks on stage carrying the tray. It is important that no one can see the nappy inside the bowl.

10 You take the jug of liquid, hold it aloft and slowly pour it into the bowl. Unknown to your audience, the liquid is being absorbed by the nappy.

11 Give the jug to your assistant, who holds it in one hand while holding the tray with the other. Pick up the cloth, flick it open and display it front and back.

12 Cover the bowl so that the cardboard form sits precisely on top of it. You must practise this move so that it happens smoothly and without hesitation.

13 Hold on to the form between both hands as your assistant lowers the tray. The tray is allowed to fall with its underside to the audience. The bowl, with the soaked nappy inside, is safely attached and hidden by the tray.

14 Your assistant now walks offstage holding the tray and the jug while you walk forward, supposedly holding the bowl between your hands. Mime this so that it looks as though the bowl has some weight.

15 Get ready to throw the cloth in the air. Count to three.

16 On "Three!" toss the cloth high into the air.

17 Aim to catch the cloth by the corners as it comes back down, and flick it out a few times, turning it from back to front to show that it is truly empty.

18 Receive a round of applause.

tip *This is the cheapest way to make the props, but of course you could make a more professional job of it. For instance, you could attach the bowl permanently to the tray rather than using adhesive putty.*

victory cartons illusion

In the mid-1900s a magician called U.F. Grant created many illusions that could be performed using props made of cardboard cartons. One of his most successful ideas was this one, which is used by professional magicians to this day. It is a great illusion, and you should practise hard to do it justice. You will find that the boxes last longer if you reinforce the edges with brown tape.

1 Cut the top and bottom flaps off a large carton, or make one to the exact size you need from four separate pieces of double-walled corrugated cardboard taped together.

2 Now find or make a second carton, which should be about 2.5cm (1in) taller than the first. Cut off the top and bottom flaps of this too, and cut a large hole in one side, leaving a border of approximately 7.5cm (3in) all around.

3 Flatten the cartons and set them down, as shown here. The box with the hole goes at the front, with the hole concealed at the back.

secret view

4 Your assistant is hiding unseen behind the back box.

5 Pick up the front box. This is the one with a hole in one panel, so be careful not to let it show.

6 Open it out and place it next to you. Notice how the box overlaps the one behind it.

7 As you position this box your assistant sneaks carefully inside, keeping low and entering the box as quickly and quietly as possible. If you are busy positioning the box at the same time, any extra movement of the box as the assistant enters will be unnoticed.

8 Pick up the remaining box, open it and hold it up high to show the audience that it is empty.

9 This is how things look from the back at this stage.

10 Place this second box over the first. Once you have done this you can even spin both boxes right round, as long as you are careful not to lift them off the ground.

11 Finally, make a magical gesture and your assistant pops up into view.

cutting a person in two

One of the most famous illusions of all time is Sawing a Lady in Half. The first version was invented by P.T. Selbit and it was first performed in the early 1920s. In this version two ropes pass through the middle of a volunteer from the audience.

1 Prepare a pair of 2m (6ft) ropes by loosely tying them together in the centre with a loop of cotton thread.

2 Invite an audience member on to the stage to be your assistant. Give them one end of the ropes while you hold the other and tug them to prove their solidity.

secret view

3 Invite another audience member on to the stage. As they approach, readjust the ropes in your hand by exchanging the ends so that you hold the centres of both and they are looped back on themselves but held together by the thread.

secret view

4 Pass the prepared rope behind the volunteer and hand the ends to your helper. This secret view from the back clearly shows what is really happening with the ropes.

5 Bring one rope from either side in front of the volunteer and tie a single overhand knot, apparently making things even more secure.

6 This is the view of what is going on as seen from the back.

7 On a count of three, pull the ropes. The thread will snap and it will seem as if the ropes have passed right through your volunteer's body. (The reason this works is that you switch the ends at step 3 and then switch them back again by tying the knot at step 5.)

metamorphosis

This is another of the most famous illusions in the world. This simple version is a very serviceable alternative for the aspiring amateur illusionist. Like the Victory Cartons Illusion, it was introduced to the magical fraternity by U.F. Grant. Make sure that you work against a dark backdrop to avoid light spilling through the back of the box and showing through the front air holes.

1 You will need a cardboard box big enough for you to get inside. Cut out eight air holes, four in the front and four in the back. Show the box to your audience.

2 Your assistant steps into the box. The assistant must be equipped with a retractable craft knife in their pocket. ▶

3 Close the lid of the box and set about sealing it up with parcel tape, explaining what you are doing to the audience.

4 While you are sealing the top of the box, your assistant cuts through the back panel, cutting between the air holes. The noise of the tape being applied and you talking to the audience will cover the noise of your assistant cutting.

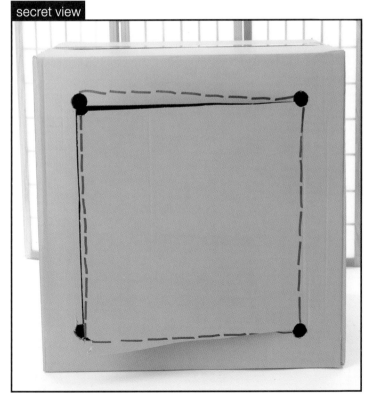

5 Arrange a screen in front of the box. From behind you can see that the hole has already been cut along three edges in the back by the assistant inside the box.

6 Stand in front of the screen and tell your audience to watch carefully. Talking will give your assistant more time, and will also help to cover any noises they may inadvertently make.

7 After about 30 seconds, walk behind the screen.

8 As you do so your assistant should be crawling out of the box.

9 Without hesitation the assistant walks round to the front of the screen as you crawl into the box.

10 The screen is immediately pushed to one side and your assistant starts to pull the tape off the box.

11 As the lid opens you stand up in the box to prove that you changed places in a split second.

tip over box

This illusion is also used by magicians the world over and is incredibly deceptive. A cardboard box is shown to be empty, but the top bursts open and the magician's assistant jumps out. You can make this style of box any size and use it to make any object appear.

1 Cut off the top and bottom flaps of a large carton if you have one, or make your own to the size you need by taping four sheets of double-walled corrugated cardboard together.

2 Cut a cardboard panel to act as a lid, and tape it on so that it will open and close with ease.

3 Cut another cardboard panel and tape it to the bottom. It is hinged along the edge that is diagonally opposite the hinge of the lid to form a flap that folds inwards.

4 Tape a strip of cardboard along the bottom edge opposite the hinge of the flap, as shown here.

5 Securely fasten a handle to the flap using tape, so that it will be on the inside of the box, and the box is ready.

6 To perform the illusion have your assistant already inside the box, with the secret flap folded up inside it.

secret view

7 Tip the box forward until the front panel reaches the floor. Your assistant stays still and holds on to the handle on the flap. The lower front edge does not move at any time.

8 From the front no one can see that your assistant is now behind the box.

9 Open the lid, which is now at the front, so that the audience can see that the box is empty.

10 This is the view of what is happening from the back.

11 Close the lid and tip the box upright again. Your assistant will now be back inside the box. ▶

12 Open the lid of the box at the top and build the suspense.

13 Your assistant makes their big entrance by jumping up and out of the box.

out of thin air

If you want to make an impact at the start of your show, this is a great way to achieve it. You show a large cloth and with a shake your assistant appears underneath. The whole illusion takes only seconds to perform but the element of surprise makes it very impressive. No one is expecting a person to appear. This trick will work with any large prop as long as it completely hides your assistant.

secret view

1 Your assistant will need to hide behind a large prop covered with a cloth. If your act includes any of the illusions in this chapter that utilize a carton, that would work well.

2 Say to the audience, "I bet you're wondering what's underneath this cloth?"

3 Pull the cloth off the prop with both hands and bring it in front of you. Position yourself so that the edge of the cloth just overlaps the edge of the box when viewed from the front. Your assistant quickly and silently crawls behind the cloth. Continue your patter, saying, "It's a box."

4 Now you raise the cloth and as you do so your assistant stands behind it.

5 This is how it looks from behind. Raise the cloth only for an instant: the faster you can make the raising and lowering of the cloth the better this illusion will look.

6 Lower the cloth with a magical flourish and say: "And this is my lovely assistant!"

putting on a show

Learning all the stunts, magic tricks and illusions in this book is one thing, but putting them together to create a show is something else entirely. Here you will find a number of things to consider before you begin this exciting task. With a little planning and a lot of rehearsal, you will soon learn to create a customized act for your next audience.

introduction

So, you've worked hard to learn a selection of the tricks in this book and have practised and rehearsed until you know your routines back to front. Have you noticed anything missing? An audience of course! Practising magic in the privacy of your own home or in front of close family or friends is good fun, but it doesn't compare to the thrill of performing in front of a live audience who are entertained, amazed and baffled by your skills.

Putting together an act or a show involves some careful planning, and there are several things you will need to consider before you can start to put a routine together. While it is not the intention here to cover all aspects of performance, you will find a number of useful tips to guide you as you start to plan your first big show.

When planning your routine you must be sure to take into account the kind of audience that will be watching. Will you be performing at a children's party or in a school? If so, how many children will be there? How old will they be? Will there be a mix of adults and children? Maybe your audience will be made up of adults only. Will you be the only act, or will there be other performers?

Why are these considerations so important? Well, children are usually entertained by things that are colourful and simple to follow, such as Blended Silks, Square Circle Production or the Unburstable Balloon. While these tricks are also entertaining for adults, an older audience also likes to see some things that are a little more sophisticated and may prefer an item such as Escapologist or Watch This! You will also need to assess and modify your patter so that is appropriate for the audience. You should avoid adult humour or subtle puns when performing to children.

The next consideration is the amount of space that will be available to you. If you are performing on a stage in a hall, for example, you can plan to include a few large-scale illusions, such as the Tip Over Box or Comedy Levitation. However, these may prove difficult or impossible if you are performing in someone's living room, where the limited space will restrict the material you can choose to include in your act.

Below: A magician entertains a large audience of children and adults at a school. Audiences of a mixed age group can be the hardest to entertain since they have different requirements.

There is no right or wrong length of time for a magic show, but you should remember the old showbiz saying: "Always leave the audience wanting more." It is far better to perform a really good 10-minute act than to work your way through a 20-minute sequence that is long winded, drawn out and has the potential to bore your audience.

If this is the first time you have put a show together, working out an act that lasts 10–15 minutes would be a good starting point. This doesn't sound like a long time, but when you are performing in front of an audience you will find that it feels quite long enough! As you build up confidence and get to know more and more material you can expand the act and make it last 20–30 minutes.

Unless you are putting on a whole evening's show, this length of act is likely to be as much as you will ever need to perform. Of course, there is nothing wrong with creating several acts so that you can choose the best one for each event, and you should always have something to fall back on should anything go wrong, such as a prop breaking at the last minute or an assistant becoming unavailable.

How should your act be shaped? It is good practice and, indeed, vital to have a strong beginning and a strong ending, and any act must be constructed with this in mind, although the bits in between are also important. Very often audiences decide whether they like an act within the first minute at most, so your opening trick or your arrival on the stage must pique their interest and create a strong impact. If you are performing for your friends and family it is likely that they will be a much more forgiving audience: as they know you anyway you won't have the additional pressure of making the spectators warm to you quickly. It may be an idea to either perform to them the first time, or at least use them as a test audience for your dress rehearsal. They will then be able to give you feedback before you face an audience of strangers.

What will you wear? Just as the contents of your show have to be well prepared, you also have to think about your costume. You may wish to don traditional evening dress, or perhaps you want to look a little more modern and opt for a more casual outfit. Either way, make sure you never look scruffy and are always presentable. You can be trendy and fashionable without looking a mess.

Above: Never underestimate the importance of first impressions and your overall appearance. A snazzy jacket, shirt and tie will complete your image and help to make you look more professional. Your outfit should reflect your individual style, however, so if your act is "in character", you will need to fit a costume that is suitable for such a character.

If you plan to send out invitations to your show, it is a great idea to set the tone and impress your audience by taking the trouble to create a magical looking invitation. You can do this very easily on a home computer by simply printing an area of black on a sheet of paper, as shown in the pictures below, and then printing the details of the show on the other side of the paper. When the paper is rolled up and secured with one or two rubber bands (preferably small black ones), the finished invitation will look like a magic wand.

Adding music before, during and after your act can help to give another dimension to the show. An exciting piece of music that builds to a crescendo before you make your big entrance is an easy way to get the audience really excited. If you are performing a mind-reading trick, some spooky music in the background can help to add a surreal and dramatic atmosphere as you probe your spectator's thoughts. You could enlist the help of a friend to start and stop the music for you, but with many mini-disc and MP3 players you can use a remote control to do it yourself.

magic wand invitations

These invitations are simple to make, impressive and functional. You could also try making other themed invitations, such as cutting the shape of a rabbit popping out of a top hat from paper and writing

on one side, or making large playing cards out of card (stock) and paper and writing or printing on one side. Allow your creativity to blossom and apply your own ideas according to the type of show.

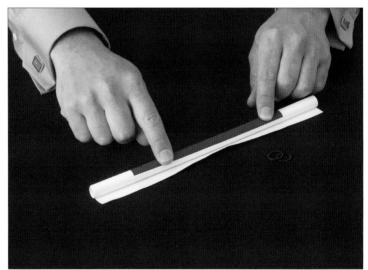

1 On a home computer, print an area of black on a sheet of paper, as shown, and then print the details of the show on the other side of the paper.

2 Roll up the paper and secure with one or two rubber bands (preferably small black ones).

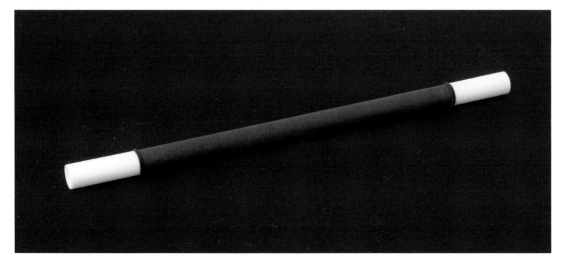

3 The finished invitation will look just like a magic wand.

setting the stage

Working out how you are going to move about the stage and where your props should be placed is known as blocking. *Make sure that during your rehearsals you are clear where all your props are* situated, *and that you can easily find them when you need them and have a place to store them after each trick is over. It is well worth having a dress rehearsal before the show.*

Screen used to hide props 'off-stage'. Ideal for props that are not to be used until later in the act.

Bowl Vanish

Victory Cartons Illusion (assistant hidden behind box).

Table set with ropes and hanky for Escapologist, book for Coin Cascade (extra coins in your pocket), Production Tube and silks for Blended Silks (Version 1).

It is considered bad practice to turn your back on the audience (unless it is a necessary part of the action). You should rehearse your moves around the stage so that you know where you will be at any given moment, and how you will get to the props you need for each trick without turning away from the spectators. This is a subtle but very important piece of advice that will help you look more professional when you are performing.

Finally, when looking at your audience ensure that you make eye contact with them. Try to look at people near the front as well as the middle, sides and back of your audience. It is all too easy to fall into the trap of looking at the same person or area throughout your show and this will distance you from the rest of the audience. Your performance should be an inclusive, interactive experience and you will want people to feel they are part of the show and that you know they are there.

Above: It's show time! Here the stage is set with every prop necessary for the act, so that you know exactly where everything is and where it is going to be placed once you have finished with it. You should always do a dress rehearsal with your assistant, if you are using one, before the show. This not only helps to settle any nerves, but means you can check everything is in place in advance.

Remember to smile and look as though you are enjoying yourself. You may well be nervous but don't let your audience see that. If you are unsure of your performance then the audience will pick up on these feelings, which will make it an uncomfortable viewing experience for them. An audience feels comfortable and relaxed when a performer is clearly in control and "at home" on the stage, so this is how you need to appear. When putting together a show there is much to think about apart from the actual tricks themselves. To give a really professional performance you will need to plan and practise your routine or act with all of the above factors in mind.

a sample act

Let's take a look at a sample show that can be created from the material in this book. This simple act will last for about 15 minutes.

After suitable music that builds to a crescendo, you make your entrance and greet your excited audience. A new music track begins – there is eager anticipation as you begin to execute your first miracle. After showing that two cardboard boxes are empty you magically produce your assistant. The crowd goes wild. The Victory Cartons illusion was a sensation.

The music continues and, as the applause subsides, your assistant ties your hands firmly together with a handkerchief in preparation for Escapologist. A long piece of rope is threaded between your arms and you prove you're a modern-day Houdini when the rope seems to melt through the handkerchief that binds your hands together. The music ends and you both take a quick bow to signify the end of that particular section of your act.

Your assistant walks off behind the screen and you thank your audience for their generous applause. Your carefully scripted patter leads you to your next miracle, Blended Silks. As you finish this neat little trick, you pass the props off-stage to your assistant in order to clear the stage of any unwanted items.

Above: Your assistant magically appears inside the Victory Cartons. This makes a great opening to an act as it introduces your assistant, as well as immediately engaging the audience with a professional-looking trick.

You invite an audience member on to the stage and perform Coin Cascade. Even though it is a close-up trick, this particular routine works very nicely for a larger audience. You are pleasantly surprised and head into your closing trick – the Bowl Vanish. Your assistant walks on-stage with the appropriate props as your music begins to kick in once more. You pour the liquid into the bowl. You pick up the bowl, walk to the front of the stage and throw the bowl high into the air. As it vanishes the music reaches its final dramatic ending, as does your act.

You take a well-deserved bow and then invite your assistant back to the stage to join you in yet another.

Your first show has been hard work but the adrenalin rushing around your body makes you feel great and you know you can't wait to perform another show soon. Your journey in magic has well and truly begun!

Left: In a demonstration of escapology you magically release yourself from the rope which is trapped around your tied wrists. Houdini would be proud of you! This is a good trick for getting the audience involved, as you not only bring one of them up on stage with you, but the rest of the audience can see from their reaction how impressive the trick is.

sample running orders

With so many tricks to choose from, it can be difficult to decide which to perform. You should consider all of the points raised in this chapter, such as the age of the audience, the venue and so on, before finally deciding which tricks are suitable. You must also, of course,

be confident that you are able to perform the tricks in a convincing manner. This means that you must practise them many times, both individually and in a running order, until you have perfected them and are confident of your patter.

stand-up show 1

| Victory Cartons Illusion |
| Houdini Outdone |
| Cutting a Person in Two |
| Crazy Spots |
| Second Sight |
| Incredible Prediction |
| Picture Perfect |
| Multiplication Sensation |
| Magic Circles |
| Bowl Vanish |

stand-up show 2

| Watch This! |
| Obedient Hanky |
| Escapologist |
| Needles Thru Balloon |
| Spiked Thumb |
| Coin Cascade |
| Anti Gravity Glasses |
| Candy Caper |
| Blended Silks (version 1) |
| Card on Wall |

close-up show

| Coin Thru Coaster |
| Vanishing Coin in Handkerchief (signed) |
| Take Cover |
| Love Match |
| Spiked Thumb |
| Marked Coin in Ball of Wool |

where to learn more

If you have enjoyed reading this book and would like to learn more, I highly recommend the following courses of action.

Visit your local library

Here you will find a number of magic books, which will range from those covering basic skills to ones suitable for an intermediate level. Using libraries is a cost effective and convenient way to learn more about the art of magic.

Join a local magic society

Once you have a basic grasp of magic and can perform a short act you will be able to prove your interest in magic is genuine and, therefore, may be eligible for membership of a local magic club or society. There are hundreds of these all over the world in practically every country, and you may be surprised at how close your local gathering is.

  Magic clubs and societies give you the opportunity to regularly meet local people with a common interest, and very often you will be able to share and trade secrets, thus greatly expanding your magical knowledge. You may also find your society has a lending library which contains a more specialized selection of magic books that are not always available in public libraries.

Above: Ping-pong Balance.

Join a magic organization

You may wish to join a more established or larger network of magicians. There are several national and international magic societies and clubs that may be of interest. Many will hold regular conventions and most will provide a regular newsletter or magazine, which will keep you up to date with everything related to that society.

Some of the biggest and most famous are listed below:

I.B.M (International Brotherhood of Magicians) www.magician.org

S.A.M (Society of American Magicians) www.magicsam.com

The Magic Castle, Hollywood, USA. www.magiccastle.com

The Magic Circle, London www.themagiccircle.co.uk

The Young Magicians Club www.theyoungmagiciansclub.co.uk

Magazines

There are many specialized magazines that you can subscribe to. These contain the latest news from the world of magic, interviews with some of the biggest names, magic tricks for you to learn, reviews of magic shows and magic tricks, as well as adverts showcasing the latest miracles you can buy.

In the UK there are two main magazines:

ABRACADABRA (The World's Only Magical Weekly)
Unit 3
Guild Road
Bromsgrove B60 2BY
www.davenportsmagic.co.uk

Above: The Bermuda Triangle.

Magicseen
Damson Cottage
South End
Seaton Ross
York YO42 4LZ
www.magicseen.co.uk

The two major US publications that are read by thousands of magicians worldwide are:

MAGIC (The Magazine for Magicians)
6220 Stevenson Way
Las Vegas, NV 89120
www.magicmagazine.com

GENII (The Conjurors' Magazine)
4200 Wisconsin Ave. NW
Suite 106-384
Washington, DC 20016
www.geniimagazine.com

Above: Straw Bottle

magic shops

All the magic shops listed allow you to buy online, although nothing can match the experience of actually visiting a magic shop in person. As well as being able to purchase the latest range of professional magic and magic-related publications, the sales assistants behind the counter will often be able to give you advice and demonstrations that would not be available if you buy on the internet.

Argentina
Bazar De Magia
Tacuari 237 -3er Piso
(1071) – Buenos Aires
www.magia.com.ar

Australia
Taylor's Magic Shop
11 Spring St, Chatswood
Sydney NSW 2067
www.taylorsmagicshop.com

Belgium
Mephisto Magic
Kloosterstraat 20
B-8510 Kortrijk (marke)
www.mephisto-magic.com

Canada
Morrissey Magic Ltd.
2477 Dufferin Street
Toronto M6B 3P9
www.morrisseymagic.com

Denmark
Pandoramagic
Damparken 30, 2th DK-2610 Rødovre
www.pandoramagic.dk

France
Mayette Magie Moderne
8 rue des Carmes, 75005 Paris
www.mayette.com

Germany
Zauber Kellerhof
Am Buschhof 24
53227 Bonn (Oberkassel)
www.zauberkellerhof.de

Stolina Magie
Hans-Böckler-Str. 50, 59302 Oelde
www.stolina.de

Hong Kong
Chu's Magic Company Limited
11/F, Flat 1-5
61-63 Au Pui Wan Street
Fo Tan, Shatin N.T. Hong Kong
www.chusmagic.com

Italy
La Porta Magica
Viale Etiopia 18, 00199 Roma
www.laportamagica.it

The Netherlands
Monnikendam
Gedempte Raamgracht 1-9
2011 WE Haarlem
Holland
www.monnikendam.nl

Spain
Magia Cadabra
Calle Navarros 7, Seville
www.magiacadabra.com

Sweden
Gycklaren Magic Marketing AB
Magic Center, Åldersstigen 2
Halmstad, Sweden
www.gycklaren.com

El Duco's Magic
Box 310 52, 200 49 Malmö, Sweden
www.el-duco.se

Switzerland
ZauberLaden Zurich
Hoerbi Kull
Rieterstr. 102
CH 8002 Zurich
www.zauberladen.com

UK
Davenport's Magic
7 Charing Cross Underground Arcade
The Strand, London WC2N 4HZ
www.davenportsmagic.co.uk

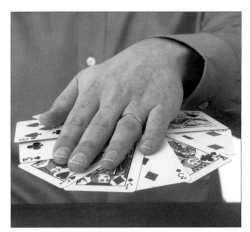

Above: Magnetic Cards.

International Magic,
89 Clerkenwell Road
London EC1R 5BX
www.internationalmagic.com

Alakazam Magic
Unit 113, Ellingham Ind. Estate
Ellingham Way, Ashford, TN23 6LZ
www.alakazam.co.uk

USA
Hank Lee's Magic Factory
112 South Street, Boston, MA 02111
www.magicfact.com

Hocus Pocus Magic
1492 N. Clark #104, Fresno CA 93703
www.hocus-pocus.com

Steven's Magic Emporium
2520 E. Douglas Ave.
Wichita, Kansas 67214-4514
www.stevensmagic.com

Worldwide
Marvin's Magic
www.marvinsmagic.com

These details are correct at the time of publication, but for the latest information and direct links to these and many other online magic shops visit **www.teachmetricks.com**
 Here you can contact Nicholas, and find further information about many of the magic tricks in this book.

glossary

There are many specialist words used within the magic fraternity. The meanings of some of the most common terms are explained here.

Cabaret magic
A stand-up act, generally viewed from at least three sides and for a large crowd of people.

Close-up magic
The performance of magic shown very close to the audience, often using small, everyday items.

Deck
A pack of playing cards.

False shuffle
A shuffle that does not change the order of one or more cards. Also used to reposition particular cards to other locations in the deck.

Force
The action of influencing a spectator's choice. The spectator believes that their choice was fair.

Gimmick
Sometimes known as a "fake". A secret tool employed, often unseen, to cause the trick to work.

Glimpse
To take a secret look at a card in the deck.

Above: Pepper-sepper-ation

Illusion
A term that generally refers to large-scale magic tricks designed for a large audience.

Lapping
A technique used to secretly ditch objects in the lap. Always performed at a table and often used as a method for the disappearance of an object.

Manipulation
Any form of manual skill, but usually associated with the highly skilful performance of sleight-of-hand on stage, such as the production of playing cards.

Method
The secret workings of a trick.

Misdirection
The skill of focusing the minds or eyes of the audience on a particular point while secretly doing something.

Optical illusion
An image that is distorted to create an untrue picture of what is being viewed, thus deceiving the eye. The impossibility of the optical illusion leads people to disbelieve or misinterpret what their eyes are showing them.

Overhand shuffle
A popular way to shuffle cards. By squeezing the front and back card every time you lift a batch to "shuffle" them, you ensure that the chosen card stays at the back of the pack.

Palming
The secretion of an object in the hand.

Patter
The banter that accompanies the performance. This is an important aid to "misdirection".

Pinch vanish
A technique used to make an object disappear from view by pinching it so it is hidden by your fingers.

Pull
A gimmick made from elastic that pulls an object out of sight.

Routine
One whole trick or a series of tricks which lead from one to another.

Silk
A piece of silk fine enough to be folded and squeezed into a small space and thus easily hidden. Silks come in all sizes and colours.

Sleeving
The secret action of hiding an object in the sleeve.

Sleight-of-hand
The secret manipulation of an object. Often associated with close-up magic, but also very relevant to larger acts.

Slide
A tube that is used to position an object in an impossible location.

Stage magic
An act performed on stage for a large audience, often using large props and illusions.

Stooge
A secret confederate in the audience who helps to make the magic happen.

Torn and restored (T&R)
When a magician tears an object, such as a card or a piece of paper, into small pieces and then "restores" it, making it whole again.

Vanish
To make an object disappear.

index

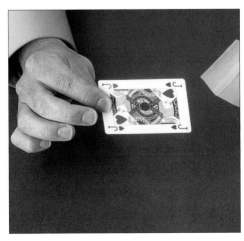

Above: Escaping Jack

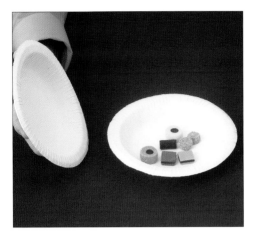

Above: Sweet Tooth

Above: Magic Papers

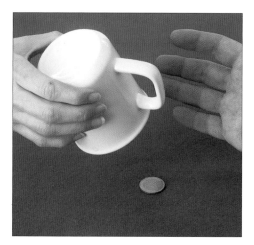
Above: Mugged Again

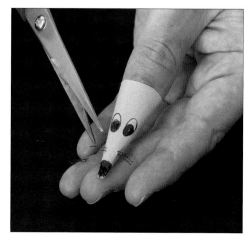
Above: Finger Mouse

Above: Love Match

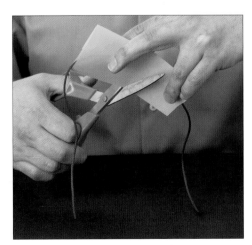

Above: Indestructable String

Above: Coin Through Coaster

Above: Clip the Queen

acknowledgements

The author would like to thank the following who either provided inspiration for some of the magic tricks herein or who assisted in the process of writing this book: Jon Allen, Eddie Ahern, Martin Gardner, Scott Penrose, Bob Loomis, Ali Bongo, Andrew Murray, Alan Alan, Adam Keisner, James Freedman, Michael Ammar, Barry Shapiro, Roy Lee, Jeff Salmon, Bob Read, Tom Mullica, David Hambly, Barrie Richardson, Robert Neale, David Britland, Martin Breese, Tommy Wonder, Oswald Rae, Alan Shaxon, Peter Monticup, Slydini, U. F. Grant, The Magic Circle, Blue Star NC.

Above: Origami Rose

The playing cards used on pages 121 and 256 are Bicycle playing cards. Bicycle is a registered trademark of The United States Playing Cards Company, www.usplayingcard.com. All other cards are Atlantis or Stratus cards. Atlantis and Stratus, the Atlantis and Stratus logo and the Atlantis and Stratus Back Design are all registered trademarks of Cartamundi Ltd. and are used with permission.

Picture credits

The publisher would like to thank the following for the use of their pictures in the book (l=left, r=right, t=top, b=bottom).

Alamy: 7b, 9, 73t, 127tl, 220t, 244; *Michael Ammar*: 13; *Frank Bemelman*: 13; *Corbis*: 6, 7t, 72t, 73b, 106, 127tr, 173bl, 220b, 221, 222, 223; *Mary Evans Picture Library*: 172; *Rex Features* 12, 107b, 173; *Jeff Scanlan*: 126 (www.bottlemagic.com).

Every effort has been made to acknowledge all of the pictures properly; however, we apologize if there are any unintentional omissions, which will be corrected in later editions.

Publisher: Joanna Lorenz
Senior Managing Editor:
  Conor Kilgallon
Project Editor: Lucy Doncaster
Editor: Beverley Jollands
Photography: Paul Bricknell
Models: Aaron Barrie,
  Lucy Doncaster and Nick Einhorn
Designer: Design Principles
Production Controller:
  Don Campaniello

A CIP catalogue record for this book is available from the British Library.

Bracketed terms are intended for American readers.

Some of the projects in this book use candles. Take care to ensure that candles are firmly secured and that lighted candles are never left unattended.

The author and publishers have made every effort to ensure that all instructions contained within this book are accurate and safe, and cannot accept liability for any resulting injury, damage or loss to persons or property, however it may arise. Matches and rope should be used with caution.